SPEAKING AND BEING

SPEAKING AND BEING

How Language Binds and Frees Us

KÜBRA GÜMÜŞAY

Translated from the German by Gesche Ipsen

P

PROFILE BOOKS

First published in Great Britain in 2022 by
Profile Books Ltd
29 Cloth Fair
London
ECIA 7JQ

www.profilebooks.com

First published in Germany as *Sprache und Sein*

The translation of this work was supported by
a grant from the Goethe-Institut.

1 3 5 7 9 10 8 6 4 2

Typeset in Sabon by MacGuru Ltd
Printed and bound in Great Britain by Clays Ltd, Elcograf S.p.A.

A CIP catalogue record for this book is available
from the British Library.

ISBN 978 1 78816 849 6
eISBN 978 1 78283 873 9

To those who paved the way for us. To those who were never seen, never allowed to fully be.

To the child who gently took me by the hand and led me through the world.

Contents

Out beyond ideas of rightdoing and
wrongdoing, there is a field.
I will meet you there.

Rumi[1]

At the very best, a mind enclosed in language is in prison.
It is limited to the number of relations which words
can make simultaneously present to it; and remains in
ignorance of thoughts which involve the combination of
a greater number. These thoughts are outside language,
they are unformulable, although they are perfectly
rigorous and clear and although every one of the
relations they involve is capable of precise expression in
words. So the mind moves in a closed space of partial
truth, which may be larger or smaller, without ever
being able so much as to glance at what is outside.

Simone Weil, Selected Essays, 1934–1943[2]

1

The Power of Language

What came first: language or perception?

On a warm summer's night many years ago, in the harbour of a small town in south-west Turkey, we were drinking black tea and shelling salted sunflower seeds with languid rapidity. My aunt gazed at the sea, into the deep, calm darkness, and said: 'Look how bright that *yakamoz* is!' I followed her eyes, but couldn't see a bright light anywhere. 'Where?' I asked. Again she pointed towards the sea, but I still couldn't work out what she meant. Laughing, my parents explained the meaning of the word *yakamoz*: it describes the moon's reflection on the water.[1] And now I, too, saw it shining brightly in the darkness ahead of me. *Yakamoz*.

I now see it every time I go for a nocturnal stroll by the sea, and wonder, do the other people around me see it too? Even those who don't know the word *yakamoz*? Because language changes our perception: I know the word, so I perceive what it names.

If you speak a second language, you can doubtless think of numerous terms that describe phenomena, situations or emotions for which there is no direct English counterpart. The Japanese word *komorebi* describes sunlight shimmering through the leaves. *Gurfa*, an Arabic word, is the amount of water you can cup in the palm of your hand. The Greek word *meraki* describes the ardent passion, love and energy with which someone devotes themselves to a task. And picture this: you are walking through an unfamiliar city, and someone gives you directions; you listen carefully, but no sooner have you set off again than you realise you've already forgotten what they said. Hawaiian has a word for it: *akihi*.

And then there's the Turkish word *gurbet*.

I was listening to the radio one morning, years ago, when I was living in Oxford. It was Eid. The presenter described the fathers making their way to mosque at dawn, the palpable excitement in people's homes, the final preparations for the communal breakfast, and the children dancing with anticipation around their gift bags in their new clothes and with freshly combed hair. The familiar sounds coming from the radio filled our kitchen – and for the first time since leaving my family in Germany to travel the world I felt the void this had created: I realised that I was missing the people back home, my parents and siblings, my grandparents, my aunts and uncles, my cousins, the community elders who would embrace me and tell me what I was like as a child, and talk about how time flies. All the people who loved me, just because. I was mourning their absence.

Although it wasn't *they* who were absent, but *I*. I had left, I was living in *gurbet*.

When I sat down at my desk and tried to put my feelings into words, my fingers danced across the keyboard. The words came naturally, fluently. Only much later did I realise to my surprise that I'd written in Turkish, even though in those days I usually talked and thought in either German or English. However, that feeling I had – the deep yearning in a strange land – was best expressed by the Turkish word *gurbet*. Were I to render it as 'living in a strange land', it would be but a poor description of what this word evokes in me.[2]

Gurbet is one of the many terms I find hard to translate into German and English, just as there are some ideas that I can articulate in English that get lost in German – like 'serendipity' or 'no-brainer' – and some thoughts that I can formulate in German but can't express in a simple Turkish sentence. Sometimes I want to say *doch* in Turkish – and in English, for that matter (it is such a fun word, which you can use to counter any argument) – at other times, I want to explain my recurrent *Fernweh* ('wanderlust'), or 'schadenfreude'; but I have to produce entire sentences before I can even begin to convey to my interlocutor what I think, mean or feel when I use those words. Some feelings live only in certain languages. Language opens up the world and in the very same instant circumscribes it.

Wilhelm von Humboldt once said that inside each language there lies 'an idiosyncratic world view'.[3] If that's the case, how much does the way one language conceives of the world differ from that of another? The fact that language – and I don't mean just words – influences our perception of the world is no longer disputed. The question that divides opinion is, rather: *to what extent* does language influence our thoughts and perceptions?[4]

Take numbers, for example: there are languages that

don't have numbers, such as that of the Pirahã, a people living in the Brazilian Amazon. Except for 'one', 'two' and 'many',[5] it has no terms to describe amounts.[6] Do the Pirahã see the world differently from us, then? In order to find out, researchers conducted an experiment: they placed up to ten batteries on a table, and asked volunteers to put exactly the same number on the table too. When there were up to three batteries on the table, they did it with ease; but when there were four or more, they became increasingly vague in their response.

Pirahãn also doesn't have special words for colours. The linguist Daniel Everett, who studied the language for thirty years,[7] reported that at some point the Pirahã simply started listing random colour words, in order to satisfy the researchers. They don't have a past tense, either: according to Everett, they therefore actually live in the moment, focused on the present – the principle *carpe diem* is prescribed to them by their language, so to speak. Only few Pirahã remember the names of their grandparents; and while other peoples living in similar circumstances produce, for instance, stores of flour to last them several months, the Pirahã only store up enough supplies for a few days at most. Furthermore, like other Amazon peoples, they have no creation myth. If you ask them what was there before – before the Pirahã, before the forest – they reply that it has always been like this. As Everett explains, the word *xibipíío* is the key to understanding the Pirahã's conceptual world:

> Eventually, I realized that this term referred to what I call experiential liminality, the act of just entering or

leaving perception, that is, a being on the boundaries of experience. A flickering flame is a flame that repeatedly comes and goes out of experience or perception. [...] Declarative Pirahã utterances contain only assertions related directly to the moment of speech, either experienced by the speaker, or [...] witnessed by someone alive during the lifetime of the speaker.[8]

For the first few years, Everett lived among the Pirahã as an evangelical missionary; but his repeated efforts to 'convert' them came to nothing. They simply weren't interested in stories from the Bible and thought it odd that Everett kept telling them about Jesus, whose deeds no living soul could testify to – for their culture is not only devoid of creation myths, but has no folk tales or oral traditions of any kind. Living with them eventually turned Everett, the missionary, into an atheist.

If we spoke a language that knew no past, would our thoughts be as preoccupied as they are with things that happened long ago? Would we indulge in historical narratives and in other people's memories? What would it mean for religions, movements and nations? If there is no collective history, are nation states even possible?

*

A nation that keeps one eye on the past is wise.
A nation that keeps two eyes on the past is blind.

Inscription on a wall in Belfast[9]

Language also influences our perception of the present. The grammar of some languages – German and Spanish, for example – assigns sexes to nouns. The word for 'bridge' is thus feminine in German and masculine in Spanish, which in turn 'genders' the descriptions of actual bridges: in German, bridges tend to be described as 'beautiful', 'elegant', 'fragile', 'peaceful', 'pretty' and 'slender'; in Spanish, however, they're usually described as 'large', 'dangerous', 'long', 'strong', 'stable' and 'powerful'.[10]

On the other hand, many languages – such as Indonesian, Turkish, Japanese, Finnish and Farsi – have no gender-specific pronouns *at all*, no 'he', 'she' or 'it'. The cognitive scientist Lera Boroditsky describes a conversation she had with someone whose native language was Indonesian: they were talking, in Indonesian, about a friend of Boroditsky's; her interlocutor, who didn't know her friend, asked Boroditsky all sorts of questions about her friend, but it wasn't until their twenty-first question that they asked her whether the friend was a man or a woman. Boroditsky was surprised. Was it possible that her interlocutor had spent the entire conversation imagining a person of undetermined gender?[11] And how about you: would you be able to listen to a story about someone, ask follow-up questions and even imagine this person, without an urge to know their gender?[12]

The language of the Thaayorre in northern Australia is particularly interesting when it comes to the perception of space and time. Kuuk Thaayorre has no word for *left* or *right*; instead, the Thaayorre use cardinal directions. They say, for example, 'There's an ant on your north-western arm,' or, 'Can you move the cup south-south-east, please?' The Thaayorre can indicate precise cardinal directions, even when in a completely enclosed space, by the age of four or five.[13] When two Thaayorre meet, their greeting involves asking the other where they are going – even in small talk, then, speakers are encouraged to name the cardinal directions, which are an elementary and inherent constituent of their language and perception. Lera Boroditsky says that when she tried to learn Kuuk Thaayorre,

I had this cool experience […]. You know, I was trying to stay oriented because people were treating me like I was pretty stupid for not being oriented, and that hurt. And so I was trying to keep track of which way is which.

And one day, I was walking along, and I was just staring at the ground. And all of a sudden I noticed that there was a new window that had popped up in my mind, and it was like a little bird's-eye view of the landscape that I was walking through, and I was a little red dot that was moving across the landscape. And then, when I turned, this little window stayed locked on the landscape, but it turned in my mind's eye. And […] I thought, oh, this makes it so much easier. Now I can stay oriented.

When she told a Thaayorre about this strange experience (strange for her, that is), 'they said, "Well, of course. How else would you do it?"'[14]

With its grammatical structures, rules and norms, our

language influences not only our perception of space and time, but also our perception of how time moves. How does time pass for you? If I asked you, as an English speaker, to put pictures of someone in chronological order, you would arrange them from left to right, starting with the childhood photos. In English, German and all Romance languages, we write and read from left to right, and that is how we perceive time. Speakers of Hebrew or Arabic would do the opposite, i.e. arrange the images from right to left. But how would the Thaayorre arrange those pictures? From left to right, right to left, leading away from their body or leading towards it – depending on which direction they were facing. Because for the Thaayorre time flows from east to west, following the path of the sun. So if someone were sitting facing north, they would lay out the pictures from right to left, and if they were facing south they would lay them out left to right.[15]

Discovering this perception of time and the world has left a lasting impression on me. Only by comparison can we discern the world view that we've been taught: everything revolves around us – or rather, it revolves around the 'I' and individual perception. I turn, and the world turns with me. What if we spoke a language like Kuuk Thaayorre, which would for ever remind us that we are nothing but a tiny dot on a gigantic map; that time flows over us, regardless of where the 'I' is? What principles, what humility would characterise our attitude to other people, to living creatures, to nature?

*

Studying another language can reveal to us the limits of our own – but we can discover those limits in a less round-about way too. You can sense the insufficiency of language, encounter the limits of your language, even without look-ing at it as an outsider. Picture the following: a father and his son are in a car, and there's an accident. Both are badly injured; the father dies on the way to hospital. The son needs an emergency operation, but, on seeing the boy, the surgeon on duty grows pale and says, 'I can't operate on him – he's my son.' Who is this person?

The educational scientist Annabell Preussler uses the riddle to show the degree to which certain images are rooted in our mind because of how we use language.[16] (Answer: the surgeon is the boy's mother.)[17]

Why does this riddle cause irritation at first? Because when we talk of a 'surgeon' we imagine a man, not a woman. We do this in English because, even though the word masks the gender of who is doing it, we have an expectation of what the journalist and feminist Caroline Criado Perez terms 'the male default'[18] – unless specified otherwise (a 'female surgeon', for example), we assume that the surgeon is male. This happens with even greater force in German, which has not only gender-specific pronouns, but also a *genus*, i.e. a grammatical sex – unlike English, for instance, where a 'teacher' can technically be female or male. Yet although German often has distinct terms for each gender, such as *Lehrerin* for a female teacher and *Lehrer* for a male teacher, it also has the so-called generic masculine, which means that a job title such as 'surgeon' includes both men and women, while still being an explicitly masculine word.

This means that the real gender of the person, or people, is further obscured, and the male privileged at the expense of the female – a problem also encountered in other gendered languages, like Spanish or French.

The linguist Peter Eisenberg argues that, in German, this kind of collective noun means *neither* men *nor* women[19] – the word 'surgeon' means simply anyone who performs surgery, and the only point of interest is the activity itself. But in that case the male standpoint is universalised, and the masculine form becomes the standard. If neither men nor women are meant, why not use the feminine form of the word? This is what Luise F. Pusch, one of the founders of feminist linguistics in Germany, proposes. This applies in English too: if the job title of the person who serves you in a restaurant were 'waitress', would it still describe everyone who does the job?

This thought experiment shows how insufficient the generic masculine is. It isn't enough for women to be – possibly – included, if they aren't at the same time imagined by whoever uses the term.

The social scientists Dagmar Stahlberg, Sabine Sczesny and Friederike Braun demonstrated the influence of gender-sensitive language on our thinking with an experiment in which fifty women and forty-six men, divided into three groups, were asked to fill in a questionnaire. The questionnaires were all exactly the same, except in terms of how they designated genders: for instance, while one group was asked about their favourite *hero* in fiction, the second group was asked about their favourite fictional *character*, and the third about their favourite romantic *hero(in)es* – i.e. using the masculine, gender-neutral and 'and/or' forms respectively.

Fictional *heroines* were named most often in the gen-der-neutral and 'and/or' questionnaires – distinctly less often by the first group, whose questionnaire used the mas-culine form, which isn't supposed to differentiate between genders. Many similar studies dealing with the use of masculine linguistic forms have produced the same result: when we use them, we think less often of women.[20]

How to solve this problem? In some countries where gendered languages are spoken, this question has been debated for decades. Should parentheses be used, as in 'hero(ine)' (thereby cementing the representation of gender as a binary either/or)? Or a slash ('hero/heroine', 'hero/ine')? How would those compound words be pronounced? Which would enter common usage? None-theless, the question remains: do suggestions such as these merely treat the symptoms? Do these languages perhaps need a new, visibly not neutral, masculine ending, so that *Lehrer* really means all those who teach in German, or *chirurgiens* really means all those who perform surgery in French – and a man is no longer seen as the standard? Or should those languages entirely do away with categoris-ing people according to gender? There are some that do this – Swahili, Uzbek, Armenian, Finnish and Turkish, for example.

I generally talk to my son in Turkish, which uses *o* in place of 'he', 'she' and 'it';[21] as my son started speaking more German, I would catch myself correcting him when he used the 'wrong' gender – of course, I was only correct-ing his linguistic mistakes, but I had to ask myself: why am I raising him to classify people first and foremost as either male or female, even before considering their more important qualities?[22]

In order to be able to express what *is*, in order to *be* who we are, in order to *see* who other people are, we have to work on the architecture of the language that is supposed to capture our reality.

*

The limits of my language mean the limits of my world.

Ludwig Wittgenstein, Tractatus Logico-Philosophicus[23]

I once talked over dinner with a diverse group about how language can discriminate against people. Many of the others around the table agreed with me, and reported their own experiences; but then a woman spoke up and said she was surprised that some of us were so interested in the subject of injustice in language. She had never considered herself excluded from the generic masculine, had never felt limited by language. On the contrary, she'd been taught to see the world in a positive light. After all, what could happen to her? Even in the worst-case scenario, she would still have a warm home, clothes to wear and enough to eat.

I wasn't quite sure what to think. I wondered whether someone who has never run into a wall, who has never plummeted into powerlessness, loss of control, humiliation, loneliness or speechlessness – whether maybe someone like that can't imagine the walls that cut through society. Maybe someone like that walks in the shadow of those walls without even noticing them, without suspecting that for many other people – whose 'worst-case scenario' would look very different – the walls are real.

The US author David Foster Wallace's famous fish allegory perfectly sums up what language and power mean to me: 'There are these two young fish swimming along, and they happen to meet an older fish swimming the other way, who nods at them and says, "Morning, boys, how's the water?" And the two young fish swim on for a bit, and then eventually one of them looks over at the other and goes, "What the hell is water?"'[24]

To humans, language in all its facets – its vocabulary, word forms, tenses – is as water to fish. It is the stuff our thoughts and lives are made of, which moulds us and influences us without our being fully aware of it. When I become conscious of it, when I sense the limits of my own perception, I feel humility – humility in the face of a world that I have been apprehending only from my own limited point of view. Knowing the existence of these limits, I am grateful: I hope that they'll prevent me from looking at the world only in the light of immutable principles and assumptions. Knowing our limits relativises the things that we, in our ignorance, assume – the things we postulate as being universal, but which in fact define nothing but the limits of our horizon.

However, the limitedness of my perception also acts as an incentive; it shows how much I still have to learn, absorb and understand. If language fundamentally guides our way of seeing the world – and thus also restricts it – then it isn't trivial, it isn't a mere political sideshow. If it is the stuff our thoughts and lives are made of, we naturally should keep asking ourselves whether we agree with how it shapes us.

You can tell a lot about our societies and cultures from how we value different languages, how we deal with perspectives beyond our own linguistic horizon, which languages are encouraged in our school playgrounds and which are scorned; you can tell a lot, too, from our attitude towards those who try to expand our language to make it more inclusive, and towards those who create words to dehumanise others.

Language is powerful. And with power comes responsibility.

How to handle such power? At moments like this, I miss the Turkish word *aciziyet*.

'Weakness', 'helplessness', 'inability' – these are the words offered by translation engines when I search for the English equivalent. But *aciziyet* means so much more. It's a word that makes me look at the world from below, from the very bottom; it makes me feel powerlessness and weakness, the absence of opportunity, that things are out of reach – and bear them all. Yet I don't think of it as a negative term; there is an odd freedom associated with it, because *aciziyet* also evokes the mindful perception of a situation to which you are exposed, an emancipated acceptance of your circumstances. Not a humiliating submissiveness, but respectful regard. Perhaps the mindful, emancipated consciousness of our nothingness is one of the few truths we can wholly comprehend. Our *aciziyet*.

When language works well for us, we don't notice the

stuff our thoughts are made of or perceive its architecture. We only sense the walls and limits of language when it no longer works, when it restricts us. When it takes our breath away.

The moment when language no longer worked for *me* was the moment I started to perceive its structure. I realised what it was that had me cornered, what was making me feel as if I was choking. Language is just as rich and poor, limited and expansive, open and prejudiced as the people who use it.

In his 1960 essay 'The Hollow Miracle', the literary theorist, philosopher and Holocaust survivor George Steiner wrote: 'Everything forgets. But not language. When it has been injected with falsehood, only the most drastic truth can cleanse it.' Steiner was referring to the language of post-war Germany; he regretted the fact that this process hadn't happened there, that the German language was instead marked by 'dissimulation and deliberate forgetting'.[25] In this, he was concerned not with language as such, but with how it shapes thought and action, with the 'relations between language and political inhumanity'.[26]

'The relations between language and political inhumanity' – that is what this book is about. It is also about how we might speak differently, more humanely. Kurt Tucholsky called language a weapon. Yes, it may be that, and is that much too often, even if those who use it aren't conscious of the fact. But it needn't be. Language can also be a tool. It can show us the luminous reflection of moonlight in the darkness of night. Language can limit our world – but also reveal its infinity.

2

Between Languages

One language, one person.
Two languages, two people.

Turkish saying

Who are we, in the languages we speak?

People who feel at home in two or more languages often report that they have a different personality in each of them. Is that possible? Are we, as the Turkish saying has it, another person – do we, as a Czech saying puts it, even acquire a new soul with each language we learn?

I speak, write and think in three languages, and feel in four. How quickly I speak, my tone of voice and my state of mind change from language to language.

I write poems in Turkish. I pray in Turkish. I cry in Turkish. It is the language whose sound was familiar to me even before I was born; it is the language in which I was loved by my mother, my father, my family – and the language in which I first loved; but it is also the language in which I first learnt to read and write. Its words connected me to my mother's world: she would sit up late into the night reading and writing, and to this day she creates poems that recast her feelings, her thoughts and her pain, simultaneously concealing and revealing them. The first novel I ever read was in Turkish, and it remains the language that can move my body and soul with just a few keystrokes. Today it is also the language in which I love my son and open up the world to him.

Today, Turkish is the language into which I decamp now and again, though without making myself comfortable in it. I can't exist entirely within it, because it is a romanticised place whose dark corners and limits I have never penetrated.

The first words my grandfather ever whispered into my ear were in Arabic: the words of the azan, the Muslim call to prayer. The prayer introduced by this call is destined only to be realised for the newborn human being many decades later, when those left behind gather at their graveside. My grandfather whispered this first, soft call, which symbolises eternity and unites birth and death, into my ear, followed by a name: Kübra. This is what I was to be called, and it is what I am called.

Arabic is my constant companion in life. To me, it is a melodious language, calming and soothing. My mother's and father's recitations would fill our home and make me feel safe. And so Arabic became the second language I learnt to read, even though I have never truly understood its meanings. It remains a language whose depths are closed off to me, a melody that I feel but can't comprehend in its entirety.

I spoke my first German words with pride, sitting on a chair in the kitchen. It was the winter before I was due to start nursery, and chestnuts were roasting in the oven. *Auto, Haus, Baum* – car, house, tree. German would become my most important, comprehensive and yet ambivalent home. It opened up the big wide world to me and granted me a new autonomy. It was the language in which I made new friends. It was the key to a wealth of literature, to narratives and tales, to pasts and visions of the future. It connected me to strangers, both friendly and less friendly ones: I finally understood what those people were saying who regarded me with such loathing. Like it or not, we were connected by the German language.

I was taught and lectured in German. Things were 'correct' or 'incorrect', and there were red lines and comments in the margins. There were evaluations: the best student and the worst student. In this language I was forbidden to speak my mother tongue, which was alien to other people. As was I.

I started speaking German rapidly, more rapidly and hectically than I do nowadays. I was trying to cram as much as I could into the time I was given – in order to tell, to explain. I wanted to exist in this language with my whole being, wanted to realise myself in it, be in it. I came up against the limits of this language. Fell down. Got up. Tried again, this time with a run-up. Slammed into its walls. Stumbled over its hurdles. Got up again, flagged, foundered, got up – again and again. Ever hopeful.

When I think in German, when I express my thoughts in it, I mourn the facets that won't fit through the eye of its needle. I want to be able to express everything in it – which is something I don't demand of any other language. I play with German, fight with it, love it and revere it – all at the same time.

Then I left Germany, and switched to English. In English I'm more relaxed. It doesn't weigh as heavily on my shoulders. In it, I am free. I trust both what I say, and who I say it to – the person who is thinking along with me. I don't wrestle with the language in a desperate effort to make myself understood. I give my thoughts room, which is why poems flow so easily from my pen in the very language that I acquired last. If I can't think of a word, I invent one. I augment the language with other languages. For me, English is elastic. It invites me to entrust myself to it. But it isn't the language in whose hands I yearn with all my heart to be. It isn't the language I long for.

German is the language I want to be embraced by. So I returned to it. I didn't want to fight it any more, I simply wanted to be in it. I began to write poems in German too. I started augmenting the language of my own accord. After all, who should I ask for permission? It is not an *emanet*, a loan, an object temporarily entrusted to me; it is part of me. It belongs to me, as it belongs to all who speak it – now that I have stopped asking for permission.

For me, Turkish is the language of love and melancholy.

Arabic is a mystical, spiritual melody.

German is the language of intellect and longing.

English is the language of freedom.

*

For the author Jhumpa Lahiri, English – the language in which she has won many awards for her writing – is the exact opposite. According to Lahiri, who is originally Indian and grew up in the US,

> In a sense, I'm used to a kind of linguistic exile. My mother tongue, Bengali, is foreign in America. When you live in a country where your own language is considered foreign, you can feel a continuous sense of estrangement. You speak a secret, unknown language, lacking any correspondence to the environment. An absence that creates a distance within you.
>
> In my case, there is another distance, another schism. I don't know Bengali perfectly. I don't know how to read it or even write it. As a result, I consider my mother tongue, paradoxically, a foreign language, too.[1]

Her relationship with English is ambivalent; and it is the same for many other multilingual authors who learnt it at school. It is the language of the majority that decides who is and who isn't included. 'For practically my whole life,' Lahiri writes, 'English has represented a consuming struggle, a wrenching conflict, a continuous sense of failure that is the source of almost all my anxiety. It has represented a culture that had to be mastered, interpreted. English denotes a heavy, burdensome aspect of my past. I'm tired of it.' On a trip to Florence with her sister in her late twenties, Lahiri became drawn to Italian – it felt like the language she had always yearned for. She kept making fresh attempts to learn it, and many years later, when she was in her forties, she finally moved to Rome with her husband and children. She immersed herself in Italian, and eventually decided to write in it too. In Italian, she says, she is a 'tougher, freer writer'.[2]

That feeling of being a linguistic exile – and the way in which languages can be enriched by each other – is a key concern for many multilingual writers. The author Navid Kermani, for instance, says that

> I breathe only German, I can shape only German. With Persian, it's different. I'm more familiar with it, perhaps even emotionally more in tune with it, but my command of it isn't as good. I haven't mastered it well enough to fashion my own language out of it. But it seems to me that, here and there, it sometimes helps me to broaden, to shape, the German language.[3]

Or there is Onejiru, a musician who grew up in Kenya and moved to Germany when she was thirteen. Kikuyu and Swahili, her mother tongues, were proscribed at her school in Kenya, where she was only allowed to speak English. Whenever she or her schoolmates were caught speaking their mother tongues they were punished, sometimes even beaten. English became a prison for her – while German, which she learnt only after she left Kenya, became the language of freedom. She discovered her sexuality, became a woman, grew up in German. 'In my mother tongues I am still a thirteen-year-old girl,' she told me. She still blushes whenever she hears someone speaking about sexuality in Swahili or Kikuyu.

Yet she sings in all her languages, in Kikuyu, Swahili,

German, English and French – the first, the chosen and the colonial. Each of them enables her to express very specific experiences, and if one of them were lost to her, a facet of her being would be lost with it. If she were allowed to speak only in one of those languages, she couldn't *be*.

There's an oft-cited remark attributed to Charles V: 'I speak Spanish to God, Italian to women, French to men, and German to my horse.' The authenticity of the quote is doubtful, but it aptly demonstrates the question of universality and utility when it comes to language.

The author Elif Şafak often writes her books in English first, and when they are translated into Turkish she goes over the text again. She says that 'sorrow, melancholy, lament [...] are easier to express in Turkish. Humour, irony, satire, paradox [are] much easier to express in English':

> As I commute between Turkish and English I pay attention to words that cannot be translated directly. I think about not only words and meanings, but also absences and gaps. Strangely, over the years I have come to understand that sometimes distance brings you closer, stepping out of something helps you to see that thing better. Writing in English does not pull me away from Turkey; just the opposite, it brings me closer.
>
> Every new language is an additional zone of existence. This is the century of people who dream in more than one language. If we can dream in more than one language, if our brain is perfectly comfortable with this multiplicity, then that means we can write in more than one language too, if we so wish.[4]

Like Kermani and Şafak, the author Emine Sevgi Özdamar tries to make the language in which she writes become porous to, as well as enrich, the one in which she thinks. She augments German with Turkish, playfully, freely, cheekily, and with an easy self-confidence. I admire the elegance and determination with which she does it. She gives herself the room she needs: if she wants to say *anadili* in German, she translates it literally and writes *Mutter-zunge* (which means literally 'mother tongue', but the correct German term would be *Muttersprache*, or 'mother language'). In her novel *The Bridge of the Golden Horn* she describes how her protagonist, a Turkish-born factory worker in Germany, is keen to lose her 'diamond'. For those who don't get the Turkish reference, its meaning remains a mystery for several pages – but she thus achieves an emotionally far more precise expression for what her heroine covets than if she had simply talked of losing her virginity. What resonates in her formulation is the symbolic charge imposed on the 'maidenhead' – and her character's hope that she'll be liberated from the weight of expectation once she has had sexual intercourse.[5]

If we first learn a language – i.e. the language of the majority society – at school, if our mother tongue is foreign to other people, then we enter the room as foreigners. The language we learn is *other people's* language, not *ours*. We make an effort to learn it, to *master* it and communicate in it, and at some point we perfect it, at some point we feel that it is *our* language. We may know no other language as well as the dominant one – and yet we still have to justify the fact that we are at home in this language.

We children who live in different languages can see the walls that cut through society, which seem to remain invisible to most people who only speak the dominant language. We children of two or more languages learn early on how to move along these walls, how to climb over and sometimes walk right through them.

We live on both sides of the wall and switch back and forth, hoping that those on one side can see what is happening on the other. We carry things from here to there, we run, we explain, until we're exhausted; but we also know that we can only wholly exist on both sides, that we need all our languages in order to *be*. So we open up the languages in which we live, yank at them and squeeze ourselves into them, stretch them in order that they can contain us; or else, breathless, make a break for it.

We need multiplicity of meaning, we need ambiguity, we need the freedom to be different within language.

At the same time, however, it is our ability not to diverge, to master the norm, to speak without an accent which symbolically decides the question of our belonging.

'Whenever I make a silly grammatical mistake, it's as if my intelligence as such is being questioned,' a law student once told me of her experience at university. Her mother tongue is Turkish, and although she only learnt German at school she quickly became one of the top students in her year. At university, though, she is one of the few students of colour, which makes her feel so insecure that she sometimes forgets the basic rules of grammar when she talks to people. Nowadays, she says, she'd rather say nothing.

For when marginalised people speak, it is not only their

words and thoughts that matter, but always also their fundamental belonging.[6]

*

Everyone has the right to be polyglot and to know
and use the language most conducive to
his/her personal development or social mobility.

Universal Declaration of Linguistic Rights[7]

Some foreign languages are more equal than others. Some bilingualisms are more equal than others.

When you think of bilingualism, which languages come to mind? English and French? English and German? English and Mandarin? They are all languages that look good on a CV, in the business world, at work. Prestigious languages.

Did you also think of English and Urdu? English and Gujarati? English and Arabic? English and Polish? English and Swahili? English and Turkish?

In 2018, when the British press found out that the then two-year-old Princess Charlotte chatted to her Spanish nanny in the nanny's mother tongue, the *Daily Mirror*'s headline announced that 'Princess Charlotte can already speak two languages – at age TWO'.[8] Countless British people who also grew up bilingual, but whose native language wasn't Spanish or French, but Urdu, Hindi or Polish, wondered whether the paper would have praised their talent quite as highly.

If you live in Britain and your mother tongue is German, French or Spanish, but you *don't* teach your child to speak it, people react with incomprehension and will criticise you for it. After all, other children go out of their way to learn those languages, signing up for expensive courses, spending time abroad or taking extra classes at school. Knowing languages like these – prestigious languages – is considered advantageous to your future career. To speak several of them is seen as a sign of intelligence, of having a knack for languages and generally higher cognitive abilities.

When a British child's second or third language is Urdu, Punjabi, Gujarati, Romanian, Polish, Turkish, Kurdish, Bosnian, Arabic, Farsi, Tamil, Hazaragi, Malaysian, Zulu or Jola, is this regarded as an exceptional talent to quite the same extent? Will they gain anything by it, will they win people's approval? Should they mention those languages on their CV?

When I was fourteen, we talked about our career plans in class and applied for internships. I was in no doubt about wanting to become a paediatrician, so I applied to a children's clinic. I set to work, and recapitulated my life so far: my family, my primary school and secondary school, and my achievements in arts and sports competitions. Then I saw the heading 'Languages' in the handout on how to write a CV given to us by our teacher. 'German, English, Latin,' I typed into the computer. And Turkish? Should I include my mother tongue?

Best not. I intuitively thought that Turkish somehow didn't count. I remembered what a teacher had told us at primary school: 'We don't speak Turkish here.' Turkish was a language spoken by immigrants. You don't learn Turkish, you *un*learn Turkish.

My mother loved poetry. She named one of my brothers after Mehmet Akif Ersoy, a famous Turkish poet, and when I was still little she taught me Turkish poems which I would recite at family gatherings. But no one at school, or anywhere else, cared that I could read and write Turkish as well as read and recite Arabic by the time I started nursery.

What if people had appreciated this multilingualism for what it is: a precious treasure, a boon to society? What if linguistic and cultural pluralism had been encouraged, if children's linguistic skills had not been considered a deficit?

How might bilingual children who don't speak one of the supposedly prestigious languages fare, if the books they read at school included works by authors writing in 'non-prestige' languages, such as Orhan Pamuk (Turkish), Nazik al-Mala'ika (Arabic), Hafez (Farsi), Noémia de Sousa (Portuguese), Faiz Ahmed Faiz and Ismat Chughtai (Urdu), or Marjan Kamali (Hindi), alongside Austen and Dickens?

What if the fact that these children are bilingual was recognised as a great potential rather than a disadvantage?

Perhaps then nobody would seek the reason for any lack of success in their ethnic origins, which they are taught to carry as a lifelong stigma. Perhaps they might find a path to a new kind of cultural or social self-conception – one that also encompasses other cultures and languages. Perhaps they might feel valued.

If that's the case, isn't it high time we made a start?[9]

*

What happens to us when we are no longer permitted to speak a language that allows the various facets of our being to make themselves heard and felt?

'Min vê sondê ji bo gelê Kurd û gelê Tirk xwend.' With these words, the newly elected delegate Leyla Zana concluded her swearing-in at the Turkish parliament on 6 November 1991, accompanied by angry boos and heckling from other delegates. 'Long live the Turkish–Kurdish brotherhood,' she had said, in Kurdish – at a time when Kurdish activists were being tortured in prison, Kurdish publishers were being shut down and the Kurdish population was mourning numerous innocent victims (it's worth noting that many of these forms of structural violence and oppression of the Kurdish people – and other marginalised minorities – continue to this day). Her words, however, were a peaceful, symbolic act of making people visible outside prevailing stigmas and taboos. Three years later, it was one of the reasons that Leyla Zana was sentenced to fifteen years' imprisonment.[10]

The problem was not what she had said, but that she had said it in Kurdish. When the Turkish republic was founded as a nation state, the various peoples who lived on Turkish territory were declared to be henceforth *one* people, and Turkish was made the official national language. Consequently, ethnic-minority languages – for example Greek, Kurdish, Circassian and Ladino – were suppressed. It is a policy that endures to this day. For decades, it was even illegal to speak Kurdish, which meant that Kurds often had to avoid speaking in their mother tongue even within their own four walls – although it was frequently the only language their parents spoke fluently.

In her book *Dağın Ardına Bakmak*, the Alevi Kurdish poet Bejan Matur, who was born and grew up in Turkey, reports her conversations with Kurdish people who had joined Kurdish rebel groups. In their biographies, the prohibition of the mother tongue again and again surfaces as a painful moment; as in the case of Ferhat, who is from Adıyaman, a province in south-east Turkey:

> Years later, in his college dorm, [Ferhat] placed a phone call to his mother. He hadn't heard from her in months. When his mother finally spoke to him from the phone in the community leader's house, the operator interrupted the conversation, saying, 'You're speaking a forbidden language. If you carry on, I'll have to disconnect you.' Ferhat continues: 'At first I didn't understand. But then I realised that by "forbidden language" she meant Kurdish! The woman again opened the door to my phone booth, and said: 'You're speaking a forbidden language. I'll have to disconnect you now.' Tears came to my eyes. As I tried to explain the situation to my mother, we were cut off. I cried. I felt so humiliated, it hurt so much.'[11]

In Turkey, language has long been a bone of contention in politics. The 'script revolution' or 'alphabet revolution' (*harf devrimi*) initiated in 1928 by Mustafa Kemal Atatürk, the founder of the Turkish state, abolished the Arabic script used in Ottoman Turkish and replaced it with the Latin alphabet. Some critics argue that it made thousands of scholars illiterate from one day to the next; others say that its very aim was to create a simplified language that would be accessible to the population at large, and thereby raise literacy levels. However you look at it, as a result of the change in the alphabet these days many young Turks are unable to read their ancestral texts in the original. I, who live far away in *gurbet*, may be able to decipher my great-grandfather's writings, but I can barely understand them – thus for me, too, a chasm has opened up between past and present.

The US biologist Robin Wall Kimmerer was confronted by a similar, but very much deeper chasm when she started to learn the language of her ancestors. Kimmerer is of the indigenous Citizen Potawatomi Nation, whose administrative seat is in Oklahoma. Like thousands of other children of indigenous peoples, her grandfather was torn from his family when he was nine and placed in a boarding school, where he ended up spending several years. The school forced the children to assimilate, prohibiting them from speaking their mother tongue. Many indigenous North American languages are now classed as endangered, including Potawatomi.

*

Puhpowee.
'The force which causes mushrooms to
push up from the earth overnight.'[12]

When Kimmerer first read the Potawatomi word *Puhpowee*, she was amazed that such a word even existed. As a scientist, she felt the gap that the absence of this word in other languages created not only in her, but also in science.

What happens when you use the word *Puhpowee*? How do you view the world? And another, even more important question: from what perspective do you regard the world? You look at the world from the perspective of the earth. Not from above, looking down at the plants that grow up to meet you, the human being, but from below, from the very bottom. You look at the world from the earth's perspective, up into the sky, past the human beings who believe themselves to be at the very centre of the world.

Would we speak differently if we lived in a language that reveals the world to us from the earth's viewpoint? A language like that of the Citizen Potawatomi, in which a plant is not spoken of disparagingly as 'it' but referred to with the same respect as humans, because it is understood as a living being which also has a perspective on this world?[13] How would our perception change? Would we live differently? How would our relationship with the earth, with nature, change?

In an interview, Kimmerer described what happened when she asked her Environmental Science students the following question: do you love the earth?

They wholeheartedly agree that they love the earth. But when I ask them the question [...] 'Does the earth love you back?' there's a great deal of hesitation and reluctance and eyes cast down, like, oh, gosh, I don't know. Are we even allowed to talk about that? That would mean that the earth had agency and that I was not an anonymous little blip on the landscape, that I was known by my home place.[14]

One summer, Kimmerer writes, all living speakers of Potawatomi came together to teach a language course. They came 'with canes, walkers, and wheelchairs'. Kimmerer counted them: 'Nine. Nine fluent speakers. In the whole world. Our language, millennia in the making, sits in those nine chairs. The words that praised creation, told the old stories, lulled my ancestors to sleep, rests today in the tongues of nine very mortal men and women.'

The mother of one man had hidden him when the children were abducted, so that he was able to remain behind as a 'carrier of the language'. He told the group: 'We're the end of the road. We are all that is left. If you young people do not learn, the language will die. The missionaries and the US government will have their victory at last.' Then, Kimmerer writes, an old woman 'pushes her walker up close to the microphone. "It's not just the words that will be lost. The language is the heart of our culture; it holds our thoughts, our way of seeing the world. It's too beautiful for English to explain."'[15]

*

What happens to people who speak a language that doesn't envisage them *as speakers*? In 1924, the Jewish German journalist and editor Kurt Tucholsky wrote – under the pseudonym Ignaz Wrobel – about an encounter he had with a Turkish man in Paris. The man spoke fluent French,

English and German. The longer the man conversed with him in German, Tucholsky writes, 'the less I paid attention to what he was saying – and by the end I well-nigh couldn't believe my ears. Where had I heard that jargon before? What was this language that he was speaking?' Tucholsky describes his nasal twang, the way he swallowed his endings, 'the tone of contempt too lazy to open its gob properly'. And then it dawns on him: the man had learnt German as a translator in the Turkish army,

> and through his German, as through a veil, appeared those who had taught him this delightful grammar, with their high collars, monocles, pink faces, the obligatory list of 'harem' addresses in the breast pocket, bedecked in German, Austrian and Turkish medals, all that full-dress frippery.

'The Turk' wasn't speaking just *any* German, he was speaking the German of the German military elite. What is so absurd, then, and both comic and tragic, is that he has the same lazy, arrogant drawl as the military officers who would never condescend to enunciate words properly for the sake of a 'mere Turk'. He talks the way they talk about him when he isn't in the room; yet it is *their* German that he speaks – fluently and confidently.[16]

*

Is German my language too? Can it include me too, and others like me?

34

Before we can answer this question, we have to acknowledge the fact that, as spoken today, German does not encompass the plurality, multifacetedness and complexity of its speakers, and that it is therefore impossible for them to speak German and at the same time convey *their* standpoint.

Take the word *Fremde*, 'foreigners', or 'strangers'. German speakers use the word not only to label people who live or come from abroad, but other German speakers whom they think of as foreigners even if they aren't, even if German is the only language in which they feel at home.

English, too, isn't innocent in its labelling: who, for example, gets to be called an 'ex-pat', who an 'immigrant', who simply, euphemistically, 'foreign-looking'? Does this language include all its speakers? Is it a home for the marginalised, the seemingly 'foreign', 'others' who do not have another language to call 'home'?

We, the 'foreigners', the 'others', therefore grow up in a language that doesn't envisage us as speakers, one that excludes our perspectives, allowing only the perspectives of those who *talk about* us, who have it in their power to categorise, label and define us, our nature and our very being.

In 1948, the author James Baldwin went into self-imposed exile in Paris: 'I left America,' he later wrote, 'because I doubted my ability to survive the fury of the colour problem here [...] I wanted to prevent myself from becoming [...] merely a Negro writer.'[17] Much of his work deals with the question of how you can write and speak in a language, and in a society, that reduces the speaker to just one facet of their being – abasing and dehumanising them. English was Baldwin's mother tongue, yet it was not the language in which he could *be*:

> My quarrel with the English language has been that the language reflected none of my experience. But now I began to see the matter in quite another way. If the language was not my own, it might be the fault of the language; but it might also be my fault. Perhaps the language was not my own because I had never attempted to use it, had only learned to imitate it. If this were so, then it might be made to bear the burden of my experience if I could find the stamina to challenge it, and me, to such a test.[18]

Baldwin adapted English to his own experience. He dared to edit it; not as a guest, but as the host. And if German isn't my language, that is my fault too. Instead of pleading with the language, begging it to make room for us, we should be taking the space we need. We should stop waiting for the day when we'll finally be free to be ourselves, and simply start being it.

Then again, I know of no 'simply' that is less simple.

3

The Political Gap

Yet it will never be mine, this language, the only one I
am thus destined to speak, as long as speech is possible
for me in life and in death; you see, never will this
language be mine. And, truth to tell, it never was.

Jacques Derrida, Monolingualism of the Other[1]

Between language and the world, there are gaps. Not
everything that *is* becomes language. Not everything that
happens finds its expression in it. Not everyone can *be* in
the language they speak – not because they are not profi-
cient in it, but because the language itself is insufficient.

Isn't it extraordinary how, by contemplating weird
symbols – *letters*, which yield *words*, which in turn form
sentences – we can plunge into other worlds; physically
still in the chair, in bed or on the train, but mentally in
places that may never have existed, inside the lives and
minds of people we don't know, with whom we suffer and
rejoice? That's the power of language; and yet this same
language can also render us speechless, because it has no
words to express our experiences, and those experiences
consequently cannot be apprehended by others – perhaps
not even by us, who have had those very experiences.

The philosopher Miranda Fricker uses the example of sexual harassment to explain what can happen if we are unable to name the abuse we experience. In the 1960s, the term 'sexual harassment' wasn't yet widespread in the US; there was no general consensus about what it described. Harassment, for example at work, was sometimes interpreted as flirting, even as a compliment: the boss who did the harassing would be unaware of any misconduct, and benefit from that lack of comprehension, while the harassed employee could neither name the event nor take measures to protect herself against it in future. Her experience did not exist. Only once the term became more widespread and there was a shared understanding of what sexual harassment constituted could the abuse be socially problematised.[2]

The disempowerment that such a 'hermeneutical lacuna' entails is substantial: those affected are unable to verbalise the problem, and the transgressors are unconscious of having done anything wrong. People thus remain both speechless and powerless, in the face of an injustice that cannot be put into words and which not enough people therefore perceive as an injustice. As a result, their reality continues to be invisible to others.

When Betty Friedan's *The Feminine Mystique* was first published in 1963, women's magazines in the US – as elsewhere – were still mostly written by men, who decided and explained how women should live and what they should feel. Men dominated academic discourse on the subject of 'the woman', developed theories about her psyche, her 'hysteria', her nature, her abilities, her weaknesses and her purpose. In a nutshell, the public image of the 'good' white suburban American woman insisted that she find total fulfilment in her role as mother and housewife, and enjoy her 'perfect life'.

When Friedan pushed back against this idea of women in her book, she was inspired not only by abstract observation but also by her own discomfort in her roles as mother, wife and wage-earner. To find out more about the structures that underpinned her discomfort she interviewed 200 women, and concluded that something was 'fundamentally wrong' with the life that she and these white women were leading in the suburbs:[3] 'There was a strange discrepancy between the reality of our lives as women and the image to which we were trying to conform, the image I came to call the feminine mystique.'[4]

She was able to formulate this discrepancy only once she had identified the structures and patterns that govern the supposedly personal, particular unhappiness of individual women – the result of observations such as the following:

On an April morning in 1959, I heard a mother of four, having coffee with four other mothers in a suburban development fifteen miles from New York, say in a tone of quiet desperation, 'the problem'. And the others knew, without words, that she was not talking about a problem with her husband, or her children, or her home. Suddenly they realized that they all shared the same problem, the problem that has no name. [...] Later, after they had picked up their children at nursery school and taken them home to nap, two of the women cried, in sheer relief, just to know they were not alone.[5]

Why did their problem have no name? Because, as Dale Spender argues, 'naming – the process of labelling, ordering, making sense of the world – is not only the province of men, but [...] also a fundamental feature of their power'.[6] Who explains the world? Who describes, who is described? Who labels and who is labelled?

*

In turning an individual perspective into an absolute, we are pursuing linguistic dominance over others.

Robert Habeck, Who We Might Be[7]

Imagine a Spaniard on the high seas, on his way to Mexico. His ship drifts off-course and he drops anchor at Portsmouth. He thinks that he has 'discovered' Mexico. Now imagine that this moment of 'discovery' enters not only his personal history, but world history, as if, before he came on the scene, there was nothing there, no history, no life, no traditions. Imagine that as a result of this 'discovery' the people of Portsmouth were not only murdered en masse and robbed of their property, but were also, their protests notwithstanding, labelled 'Mexicans'.

It would constitute an insistence on the perspective of ignorance, of violence, of murder and of colonial rule. This is exactly what we do if we describe America's indigenous peoples as 'Indians', or defend the use of the N-word by people who are not Black:[8] we perpetuate a dehumanising, coloniser's, slave driver's point of view.

To call people what they would like to be called isn't a question of being polite, nor a symbol of political correctness or a progressive attitude – it is simply a question of common decency. I refuse to call others anything other than what they would like to be called. I refuse to suppress their perspective, and instead make room for it.

There are many perspectives in this world – as many as there are people. Taken by themselves, each of them is narrow. Everyone is prone to prejudice and limited by their experience. But when certain perspectives – for example those of white Europeans or white North Americans – are privileged above others, when their narrow point of view claims the right to dominate, claims to be universal, objective and neutral, then other perspectives and experiences lose their claim to validity. It is as if they didn't exist.[9]

Yet whenever a dominant perspective and its claim to universality are scrutinised and challenged, there's an uproar. Terms such as 'mansplaining', 'manspreading' and 'gammon' encounter resistance because they reverse the perspective: the ruled are describing the rulers, and thereby not only reveal how specific and oppressive supposedly neutral attitudes can be, but illuminate the very concept of attribution. Thus old white men – perhaps for the first time ever – are being classified as a generalised type, one that is privileged without questioning its privilege, and dismissive of feminist and anti-racist positions.

Such scrutiny doesn't happen suddenly. Rather, it smoulders – for years, often decades. It happens in silen in unguarded moments; it is whispered, or understood only by those in the know, often concealed or masked by banter, jokes and laughter. Such as at the 2013 Oscars, for instance: having read out the names of the five nominees in the 'Best Actress' category, the host, Seth MacFarlane, waited for the audience's applause to die down before adding, 'Congratulations. You five ladies no longer have to pretend to be attracted to Harvey Weinstein.' The audience laughed. Four years later, in October 2017, everyone else got the 'joke': #MeToo made women's previously hidden experiences of assault visible.[10]

The internet has allowed points of view to emerge from silence and given them a voice. Without the need for one person to interview hundreds of people – as Betty Friedan had to in 1963 – it has created digital discursive spheres in which potentially millions of people can share experiences that have previously gone unnoticed and unheeded. In September 2013, thousands of Twitter users published their experiences of everyday racism using the German-language hashtag #SchauHin ('don't look away'). While political discussions about racism in Germany were predominantly limited to past events, or contemporary extreme cases like burning refugee shelters or right-wing terrorism, this hashtag highlighted racism in daily life, at school, at university, at work, on public transport, while house-hunting – experiences and events that often go unnoticed and tend to be reduced to individual cases rather than traced back to systemic and structural problems. For thousands of people in Germany and all over the world, from the UK to the US and beyond, these are everyday occurrences, events that happen so often and so casually that those who experience them at the same time learn to normalise them:

> When Grandma scrubs her grandson down in the bathtub to make his skin a bit lighter
> #schauhin (@AbrazoAlbatros)[11]

> #SchauHin when they talk about honour killings and forced marriage at your job interview, instead of about what qualifies you for the position!
> (@NeseTuefekciler)

> It's winter and my friend wants to borrow my gloves for a bit. My teacher says: 'No, she needs them herself, it's colder here than in Africa' #SchauHin
> (@Nisalahe)

#SchauHin sparked a widespread media debate about everyday racism in Germany,[12] and similar campaigns have been visible around the world: in 2017, in response to the Australian government announcing the weakening of race-hate laws, Australian Twitter users shared hundreds of stories of racism with the hashtag #FreedomOfSpeechStories.[13] In the same year, the US media's disrespectful, racist treatment of two Black women – one a journalist, the other a Congresswoman – sparked a global hashtag campaign about everyday racism, #BlackWomenAtWork.[14] More recently, in 2021, in response to a rise in hate crimes against Asian communities, the hashtag #StopAsianHate turned the spotlight on anti-Asian racism and violence.[15]

These campaigns offered yet another opportunity to make the idea of everyday racism meaningful and more widely understood, without any need for the kind of special reason usually required for us to pay attention to this aspect of society, such as burning buildings and death tolls[16] – but just because. Because everyday life is reason enough.

At the age of 10, I was at the local pool as a group of white boys held my head underwater, laughing at me for being Asian. #FreedomOfSpeech (@mrbenjaminlaw)[17]

Carload of white boys yelled 'I like your slopehead girlfriend' & chucked food at us in a Maccas carpark. #FreedomOfSpeech @mrbenjaminlaw (@squig_)[18]

Me: I'd like to check on the status of the books for this class. Staff: The faculty member does that. Me: I am faculty. #BlackWomenAtWork (@NyashaJunior)[19]

#BlackWomenAtWork my boss: your hair is making too much [sic] stat[e]ment Me: Susan's has 4 different colors. My boss: yes but it's not an afro (@LisaCraddock1)[20]

my family left nashville, my hometown, bc a white woman was so disgusted & enraged by my existence that she grabbed me by my hair, spit on me, dragged

me out of a store, & threw me into the street. i was 8.
my heart was broken then & it's broken now. please
#StopAsianHate
(@reebsthereader)

Again, I was harassed. In line for my second [Covid-
19] vaccination, a white man, older was yelling at me.
I'm on a meeting call with headphones but he's so loud
they can hear. I ask him to stop and his yelling gets
louder. No one around me spoke up or asked him to
stop. #StopAsianHate
(@YehCathery)

It's clear from their sheer number that these experiences
are not unique, or just cases of individual people being
'overly sensitive'; rather, they are part of a structural problem affecting society. When we give an injustice a name, we
make room for it and make it intelligible. Experiences no
longer remain nameless and unspeakable. When individuals confirm each other's experiences in campaigns such as
#MeToo, #SchauHin, #FreedomofSpeech, #BlackWom-
enAtWork or #StopAsianHate they raise awareness in
society, and something once visible only to those affected
by it becomes visible to outsiders too: racism, sexism, in
everyday life. Every day. All over the world.[21]

A TV editor who was working on a programme about
#SchauHin once told me that when he stopped passers-by
in the street and asked them about their experiences with
everyday racism, nearly all played it down. They said that
they had never experienced anything like that. Yet many

returned minutes later, because they'd suddenly remembered something after all. And then remembered another thing. And another. And another.

*

> If you don't move you don't notice your chains.
>
> *Attributed to Rosa Luxemburg*[22]

Why is it that the experiences and perspectives of certain groups of people rarely find their way into mainstream language – or only after a long battle? Who has the authority to label experiences, situations, events, people and groups of people?

Think of language as a place: an immense museum that explains the world out there to us. You could spend weeks, months, years, a whole lifetime in this museum. The more time you spend there, the more things you understand. It allows you to immerse yourself in worlds that you have never experienced yourself, which are neatly arranged and organised into categories and made comprehensible by means of labels and definitions. Here you'll find objects, animals and plants from every continent, as well as ideas and theories, thoughts and feelings, fantasies and dreams. Things long gone, but also highly relevant ones.

There are two categories of people in this museum: the *labelled* and the *unlabelled*.

The unlabelled are people whose existence isn't questioned. They are the standard. The norm. The yardstick. The unlabelled stroll through the Museum of Language blithely and freely, because it was made for people like them. It shows them the world from their point of view. This is no coincidence, because it is the unlabelled who curate the museum's displays. They decide what to show and what not to show, they label the objects and define them. They are unlabelled, but they make use of the power of the label. They are at the same time the *labellers*.

Yes, the Museum of Language opens up the world to us. But it by no means comprehends it in its entirety, in the fullness of its many aspects. It merely comprehends what the labellers themselves comprehend – as far as their senses and experiences go, and no further.

The other unlabelled don't notice its limitedness; they don't even notice that the way they perceive the world is guided by others. The extent to which they can move through the Museum of Language freely and blithely becomes clear only when we consider the second category of people in this museum: the labelled. At first, they are simply people who in one way or another diverge from the norm of the unlabelled, anomalies in the world of the unlabelled. Unforeseen. Strange. Different. Sometimes merely unusual, unfamiliar. They irritate. They are not *self-evident*.

The unlabelled want to understand the labelled – not as individuals, but collectively. They analyse them. Scrutinise them. Categorise them. Catalogue them. Finally, they bestow upon them a collective label, and a definition that reduces them to the features and characteristics that the unlabelled think worth noting. This is the moment that those people become the labelled – and are dehumanised.

These people – the labelled – who are now no longer people, live in glass cages, carefully categorised and tagged with their collective names. Their label creates their glass cage, and their definition defines its size: the narrower their category, the smaller their cage. We look at them through the eyes of the unlabelled: faceless beings, constituent parts of a group. Their every statement, their every action, is traced back to the collective; they are denied individuality. This doesn't strike the unlabelled who observe them as unusual – despite the fact that individuality forms the very basis of their own being.

*

In March 2015, a Germanwings plane crashed in the French Alps, killing all 150 people on board. The subsequent investigation established that the co-pilot had locked the flight captain out of the cockpit before crashing the plane. The perpetrator had suffered from depression and was suicidal.

In July 2019, a man pushed an eight-year-old boy and his mother in front of a train in Frankfurt am Main. The mother survived, the boy died. In this case, too, the perpetrator suffered from mental illness.

Yet the one perpetrator was a white German man, the other a Black man from Eritrea living in Switzerland.

What happens in the aftermath of horrific acts like these? Whose background and skin colour are discussed, whose mental illness detailed? Who will be considered a lone wolf, an individual? And who will be doomed to represent an entire continent, religion, race, category? Countless cases could be listed here – from the response to the mass shooting perpetrated by Dylann Roof in the US, where the white gunman was apprehended without being harmed, to the murder of the soldier Lee Rigby in the UK, where the coverage focused on radical Islam despite the fact that one of the attackers suffered from severe mental-health problems. How telling that when the FBI published a report on lone-wolf terrorist attacks in the US between 1972 and 2015 it turned out that 65 per cent of the perpetrators were white.[23]

The day after the murder in Frankfurt, a woman approached the anti-racism coach Sarah Shiferaw at a train station. They chatted about this and that, until the woman pointed at a Black man. 'Look how dark he is,' said the woman, and told her she was scared. So Shiferaw told her about the Black men in her own family, and asked, 'How do you think they feel? How do you think he [the man on the platform] feels? [...] They have to deal with the fact that those around them think of them as criminals, because someone somewhere [...] has committed a terrible crime.'[24]

*

When someone shows you who they are,
believe them the first time.

Maya Angelou[25]

As the unlabelled wander through the Museum of Language, they sometimes bump into labelled ones who don't appear to conform to the collective names written on their labels. A hijab-wearing punk, for instance, or a Black male ballet dancer. They run into the walls of their cages and bloody themselves on the glass; they have recognised their cage as such, have understood the fact of their imprisonment, and now threaten to leave it and walk freely through the museum, to mix with the unlabelled, unscrutinised and undefined.

This threat causes such outrage, aggression and violence that the labelled usually end up shrinking back – withdraw, afraid, into their glass cages, where they henceforth orientate themselves strictly on the collective names and definitions they have been assigned. *Who* should I be? *How* should I be? *What* should I be? Now they move only with great care, keeping well away from the glass walls, the framework of what defines them, until in the end they become caricatures of themselves. Stereotypes.

But some persist. They stand up to the upheaval, the fury, the outrage and the violence; they run into the glass undeterred, crack it, and finally squeeze themselves through into the freedom beyond. They refuse to allow these walls to constitute the limits of their existence. Yet no sooner have they broken through the glass and, for a brief moment, breathed freely, than they are scrutinised by the labellers. The labellers undress them, turn them this way and that and reassess them, every inch of their bodies, minds and souls – whatever is available for them to 'discover', explore, define and analyse. Why are you like this? Why do you look like this? Live like this? Love like this? Believe like this? And the labelled, they put up with it, because they hope that freedom awaits them on the other side. They want to escape their definitions. They want to speak freely.

Instead, they are riddled with questions about the colour of their skin, the texture of their hair, what their bodies can do, their clothes, their head coverings, their sexual organs and sexual preferences. With questions that question their intelligence, their capacity for reason, their humanity.

The key to freedom is free speech. It opens the cage; it harbours the potential to question the cages as such and the unchallenged perspective of the labellers, i.e. the Museum of Language's curators – even the layout of the museum itself. That is why the labelled are supposed to speak only when they are being scrutinised, remain silent except to answer questions. They comply because they want to explain what they are *really* like, and hope that people will then stop defining them. Patiently, they try to make themselves understood, but the questions are asked in such a way that any answer perforce validates the category.

I am one of the labelled. One who is investigated, analysed, scrutinised. One whom people, puzzled, ask – in daily life but also during conferences, panel discussions and interviews – how it fits together: Islam and feminism, hijab and emancipation, faith and education; simply because the existing categories don't apply. For years, I was one of those who put up with being scrutinised. Now I am one of those who dare to speak without being spoken to, to make glass walls visible, to name their imprisonment and end it. I am one of those who had the cheek to reverse the perspective – to label the museum and the labellers.

For years, I believed that my fight against being stereotyped would succeed at some point, that my role as an object of scrutiny was only temporary. But I no longer want to merely react, respond to questions and accusations, or right wrongs. I want to speak not because I am called on by others to speak, but because I call on myself to speak. Not to be understood, but to understand. Not to explain *myself*, but to understand what constitutes and surrounds us.

*

When they speak it is scientific, when
we speak it is unscientific;
universal / specific;
objective / subjective;
neutral / personal;
rational / emotional;
impartial / partial;
they have facts, we have opinions;
they have knowledge, we have experiences.

Grada Kilomba, Plantation Memories[26]

To assert the universality of their view of the world, the labellers label it. They call it *universal*, *neutral*, *rational*, *objective*. Their view of things carries the most powerful label of all: knowledge. It is the norm that does not need to explain itself, and which simultaneously compels all that diverges from it to explain itself – a mechanism that pervades so many social constellations. 'Whiteness and maleness are implicit,' writes Caroline Criado Perez. 'They are the default. And this reality is inescapable for anyone whose identity does not go without saying, for anyone whose needs and points of view are routinely forgotten. For anyone who is used to jarring up against a world that has not been designed around them and their needs.'[27]

The standpoint of the unlabelled thus becomes the measure of all things; we don't even notice that we are gazing upon the world, including ourselves too, through their eyes. We don't notice that we are trapped by their gaze, that we cannot *be*.

That is what happens to people who are described as 'foreign', who are robbed of their individuality, their uniqueness, their face, their humanity. That's what happens to people when they are primarily and from the first assigned collective tags: *foreigner*, *Jewish*, *Muslim*, *gay*.

A verse fragment by Paul Celan begins by enjoining the reader not to write themselves 'between worlds'. It is a poem that seems to celebrate the plurality of meanings, and ends by urging us to 'learn to live'.[28] He wrote it in France, in German, his mother's language – and that of her murderers. Whenever I read these lines, I hear in them not only a poet's warning and self-exhortation to stay alive, four years before ending his life: I also hear in them the expression of a person's longing to exist. To be in language. And to be *despite* language.

Another poet, the Turkish migrant worker Semra Ertan, wrote about racism, xenophobia, the working conditions she experienced in Germany and how she and her work were perceived there, in her 1981 poem 'Mein Name ist Ausländer' ('My name is Foreigner'). In the poem, she describes her low-paid, 'dirty' work, being told to go back where she came from, being seen not as an individual but merely as a 'foreigner'.[29]

A year later, in May 1982, Semra Ertan called in to a live show on Germany's NDR radio. 'I'm going to burn myself to death. Don't you want to report that?' she asked.[30] She explained her reason for killing herself: 'The Germans should at least not treat us like dogs. I want to be treated like a proper human being!'[31]

She did what she said she would do. Racism, exclusion, violence and rejection led to her public death at the age of twenty-five.

She, the *foreigner*, was in reality much more than that. So much more than that.

She, the labelled, fought for the right to label herself.

4

Individuality Is a Privilege

> Measure, measure, measure. We learn to measure first.
> We spend our days measuring. And when we count we
> start at one. Every number after is in relation to one.
> Two is one after one. Three is two after one. And
> so on. Every child knows that one is the beginning
> from which all other numbers arise. And every child
> knows that one is Whiteness. The beginning.
>
> *Kartina Richardson*, Salon[1]

Individuality.
  Complexity.
  Ambiguity.
  Flaws.
  Imperfections.
  All these are *privileges*.
  In reality, of course, individuality, complexity, ambiguity, flaws and imperfections aren't privileges. They make us human – we can't exist without them. Yet the very things that make us the heterogeneous creatures that we are, are privileges denied to anyone who deviates from the norm, those who are scrutinised, labelled and imprisoned by the definitions the labellers impose on them: *the* Jewish

woman, *the* Black man, *the* woman with a disability, *the* immigrant, *the* Muslim woman, *the* refugee, *the* lesbian, *the* trans woman, *the* migrant worker.

Each is labelled and viewed in terms of a category, as if it were possible to understand someone without spending time with them and seeing things from their particular point of view, without knowing their contradictions, flaws and imperfections. Even then, though, you can never truly know a person – or can you honestly say that you have completely and thoroughly understood even yourself, and that you're able to make others understand you in all your complexity and depth? Yet people who diverge from the norm are denied indeterminacy and robbed of their individuality. As far as they are concerned, complexity is a privilege.

*

In early 2019, a reader wrote a letter to a German newspaper, asking them to guess:

> Who am I? I am in the media more often than Donald Trump and his tweets, Erdoğan and his democracy or Putin and his policies. I was the main reason why attempts to form a government failed, and why the right is on the rise in Europe. For many citizens of this country, I am a key issue that needs to be resolved, because I'm a bigger threat than old-age poverty, domestic and child abuse, pollution, drug addiction, climate change or the shortage of carers and teachers. I am the one who always feels responsible for other

people's mistakes, people I don't even know. When something has once again happened somewhere, I am the one who is always too embarrassed to say hello to my neighbours. I am liable for every single person's mistakes, and feel threatened by every media report.

At the end of the letter its author, Syrian lawyer Vinda Gouma, revealed the answer: 'I am *the refugees*. And by that I mean all refugees.'[2]

There are many people who can walk the streets and just be themselves. They can be unfriendly, get angry, give their emotions free rein – and no one will draw any conclusions from this about everyone else who looks like them or practises the same faith. However, when *I*, who am visibly Muslim, cross the street at a red light, 1.9 billion Muslims are crossing the street with me. An entire world religion flouts the traffic rules with me.

When will a young woman from an immigrant background, a gay man, a refugee like Vinda Gouma, a trans woman or a person with a disability be able to just be themselves? When will they be able to say 'I' and mean 'I'? When will they be apprehended as an 'I'? Gouma writes, 'I have lost friends and relatives, my flat, my job, my car, my past and my homeland in the war. But I only realised later that I had lost my individuality too. I left it behind with the rubber dinghy on the European border.'[3]

I see young men from an immigrant background, young Black men, make a special effort to be friendly and helpful, to smile pleasantly so as not to come across as a threat – or simply in order to be seen as human.

I see young women in hijabs acting almost overly eager to please, carefree and easy-going, to prove that they aren't oppressed, but smart and friendly – or simply human.

They are the labelled ones performing under the gaze of the unlabelled, in order to be apprehended as people. You only realise how exhausting this is by comparing it to those brief moments when they are among themselves, no longer exposed to the pressure of scrutiny: when they breathe a sigh of relief, drop their guard, relax their shoulders and facial muscles, and return their carefully raised eyebrows – that deliberate I'm-not-a-threat look – to their natural position.

A young Muslim student once approached me after a talk, and told me about her activism, the resistance and discrimination she encountered, and her despair. As I looked at her, I wanted nothing more than to take the burden of *representation* from her shoulders. 'You're allowed to be *you*. You don't have to explain or justify yourself,' I told her. 'You're free. You don't have to prove to others what a Muslim woman is or can be like. Just be *yourself*, with all your quirks and foibles.' As I talked, I noticed how she opened up, how her body relaxed and her shoulders dropped. She came into focus. And then her eyes filled with tears, tears of relief but also of consciousness, of a growing awareness of the unbearable burden she was carrying around with her, day in and day out. When we hugged, it felt like I was hugging myself.

In her essay 'Muslims shouldn't have to be "good" to be granted human rights', the US journalist Sara Yasin describes what happened when she decided to stop wearing a hijab:

In the days after [...] I remember weaving through crowds, feeling drunk on my invisibility. There was an ease that came with my perceived whiteness: the world seemed more polite. Fewer people were rude to me, fewer people stared, no one asked where I was 'really from' or marveled at the fluency of my English.

Being perceived as white meant my citizenship was no longer casually called into question. I did not have to prove that I was American; I just was. But the biggest change [...] was this: I realized I didn't have to be so *nice* all the time. [...] I was suddenly viewed as an *individual* – and any rudeness on my part was mine alone. But the real question is, why wasn't that true before?[4]

The Muslim woman is a favourite object of Western curiosity – a curiosity that once found expression in those erotic harem paintings that tell us more about their painters' gaze, and the world in which they lived, than about the world of those they misrepresent.[5] And this curiosity, this obsession and this colonial gaze persist to this day. We want to know and understand who *the Muslim woman* is. In science, literature, art and journalism, she is scrutinised and categorised as if she were an animal species to be exhibited to humanity, and as if each Muslim specimen were identical to all others. Young, old, queer, white, Black, of colour, with or without a disability, refugees, workers, academics – all are robbed of their voice and their visibility.

I am a Muslim woman, one through whom other people try to understand the workings of *all other* Muslim women.

One who for years allowed herself to be scrutinised, in the hope that it would enable her to 'fight prejudice' and 'break down stereotypes'. Like all others who were scrutinised before and after me, however, I didn't gain any freedom but merely found myself in a slightly larger cage. We will only gain our humanity and our freedom when we no longer respond to questions about *the* Muslim woman, when we are given permission to be contradictory, multifaceted and un-understood.

Current discourse scrutinising *the* Muslim woman has concluded that she is generally allowed to exist in two types of cage: she's either a victim, and therefore not dangerous but herself vulnerable, for instance to a patriarchy validated by Islam, and needs to be protected from those bad Muslim men; or she herself constitutes a threat – or presages a greater threat still, in that she enables patriarchy or Islamification.

Muslim women all over the world are battling against such reasoning, and many appear to have succeeded, for example in fashion, sport, culture, science, business and politics. But unless their new roles abolish old-fashioned notions of collective identity, they merely keep creating new cages. Perhaps progressive circles will one day conceive of twenty, or a hundred, categories of Muslim women – enough, perhaps, for them no longer to be aware of the fact that they still remain caged. Perhaps they will be ennobled as 'exceptions', and isolated from the rest of their category, so that the power structures can persist undisturbed. Nevertheless, every time a Muslim woman who is different from those hitherto scrutinised takes to the stage, an anxious murmur will run through the audience; until they have found a new category, a new term, which makes her existence comprehensible to the unlabelled, until they can say, Yes, we have *understood* you – a liberal, queer, working, refugee, conservative, orthodox, Black, white, modern, highly educated, traditional Muslim.

For years, people kept asking me to write books and articles about *the* Muslim woman – or about *the* young Muslim woman in Germany, *the* modern Muslim woman, *the* feminist Muslim woman – and all those years I was never able to clearly explain my discomfort in that role. I felt as if I was suffocating, but didn't know why. Only later did I realise that, no matter how good my intentions were, any book about *the* Muslim woman that I might have written for a non-Muslim readership would have brought neither enlightenment nor freedom, but only further manifested the imprisonment of those described in it.

If I was forced to write about Muslim women, I would only have one choice: I would have to describe the walls of the cage that encompasses them and everyone else who is labelled. The women themselves cannot be described – not without naming the patriarchy, sexism, racism and all the other power structures that seek to regulate our coexistence.

*

Kathleen [...] wants to exist in all her complexity: as angry, as quiet; as strong, as weak; as joyful, as sad; as

knowing the answers, as not knowing at all. [...] And
we should feel free to allow this complexity to exist.

Grada Kilomba, Plantation Memories[6]

A stereotype is like a suit of armour. Yet instead of shield-
ing its wearer, it shields the ignorance of those on the
outside. A stereotype is like a suit of armour forged out of
ignorance, which those who are ignored are made to wear.
They weigh heavily; they are a burden to those who bear
them, and in moments of human weakness can bring them
to their knees.

I considered the stereotypes that I was threatening
to turn into: *the hijab-wearing woman, the committed
Muslim, the liberal Muslim, the feminist Muslim, the
exception.* I saw the armour my predecessors had to wear,
and the traces they left behind in their attempts to break
through it. I gathered up their emotions and heard their
calls and their songs, which still reverberated beneath the
armour. Immigrants, migrant workers and unheard witnesses, whose words were called *silence*, although they
were never mute – they merely spoke a different language.

The words of my grandmother, who learnt to read and
write at the age of seventy, are incomprehensible to others.
Her sense of humour, her intelligence, her perceptiveness –
all invisible. People look at her, but don't see her; and they
don't see her female friends either, women whose sharp
edges only make them even more likeable, women who have
witnessed poverty, suffering, death and misery, who have
experienced alienation and the brutality of social indifference. Women who clung to each other in order to *be*.

Their daughters spoke the 'right' language, but their words, too, went unheard. They were too quiet, too far removed from the centre of society. The people who were unable to see beyond the limits of their own horizon, or even to admit the existence of those limits, didn't think they mattered; so they remained imprisoned within their armour of ignorance, as if they had never spoken in the first place.

They grew up with the mantra that they had to work twice as hard as others to succeed. They had been raised to navigate their way inconspicuously and quietly through injustice and resistance, and to make no demands – after all, they were the daughters of guests, of families who sat on packed suitcases and whose children acted as their translators.

And now I look around me, at my own generation: we don't want to work twice as hard as others to achieve the same things. We want to be treated fairly. Our generation speaks and is heard, but nevertheless remains silent. Appallingly silent.

So long as we speak only when we are summoned to, and only on prescribed subjects, we will never truly speak, or ever be truly heard. We remain under scrutiny. We wear the armour.

Is a young hijab-wearing woman who has been politically engaged since she was a teenager allowed to talk about youth and politics on a TV talk show? No, said a friend of mine, the editor of a talk show to which I was once invited – though my invitation was later scrapped. Why? The host had said that 'we can't have a woman sitting here in a hijab, and not have her talk about her hijab'.

Are we actually *talking*, if we're merely a two-line soundbite, mere extras in a debate that labels us as *foreigners*, being stared at through distorted and discoloured lenses? Are we really *talking*, if we're only permitted to talk about specific topics, within a narrow scope?

When I found myself no longer able to stifle that feeling of eloquent silence and began questioning my presence at talk shows on Islam-related subjects, I was told that my contribution had been invaluable: it was because of me, for instance, that people now knew better than to think that hijab-wearing women have no voice and are oppressed. I replied that they hadn't come to that realisation because I had told them so, but because of the *very fact* that I had spoken. It was the fact that I spoke that had opened their eyes – I could just as well have talked about the reproductive process in ladybirds, or the weather forecast for the next few days. What had been decisive and new was the sight of a speaking Muslim woman.

Looking back on it, however, I think that the things I talked about may not have been irrelevant after all. Had I actually spoken about ladybirds or the weather, it would at the very least have meant that I wasn't speaking as someone under scrutiny – I would have been speaking freely.

When we are objects, we aren't speaking. When the topic is prescribed, we aren't speaking. When we are told to speak for a group, we aren't speaking.

We are speechless.

*

As soon as we learn words we find ourselves outside them.

Sheila Rowbotham, Woman's Consciousness, Man's World[7]

A few years ago a friend said to me, 'I don't get why you complain that you don't have a voice.' I, who had access to so many platforms – via Twitter, Facebook, blogs, interviews, talk shows and discussion panels – I, of all people, was complaining that I had no voice?[8] Yet that privilege means nothing if people merely see someone who does or says this or that *despite* her hijab, someone who is an entertaining exception, an object of curiosity exhibited for their diversion.

Muslim women are reduced to no other attribute as much as this one piece of clothing. They are even labelled accordingly: they are *hijab-wearers*, or *hijabis*. Their humanity and the way they experience the world are reduced to just this. It's almost unbearable, spending your life as a walking public information point for a religion and everything associated with it. Still, it's the life that so many Muslim women lead in our society. They are regularly denied jobs,[9] and prevented from entering schools[10] or certain professions.[11] Somehow, when it comes to hijab-wearing Muslim women, their individual qualifications, character and qualities appear to be irrelevant. I regularly get messages from Muslim women, young women in particular, describing their experiences. One of them wrote that 'people barely perceive me as a person. They regard me as a religion, as unapproachable, and that hurts. I don't know what to do.' They are perceived not as people, but as their religion's press officers. People introduce them to others as members of their faith, and at some point they start introducing themselves that way too – because they have been under scrutiny for so long that they're no longer conscious of their individuality, ambiguity and complexity, but have become absorbed by other people's point of view.

Maybe you, too, are wondering why I wear the hijab – just like all those people who come up to me after one of my talks about feminism, artificial intelligence, internet culture or political art. I would explain it to you, but my answer might not satisfy you, because you don't just want to hear my reasons for it, you want to *really understand* them.[12] However, nobody can spend every day constantly accounting for their complex existence, for all those circumstances, motives, changing moods and highs and lows which are incomprehensible sometimes even to themselves. At least, not without putting their humanity at risk.

The poet Anja Saleh once told me that

one can't understand everything. I don't understand why people climb mountains, but there's nothing to say that I need to. In my view, what requires real skill is not to pressurise people into making things intelligible to us so that we can put ourselves in their shoes. When someone wants to understand why I wear a hijab, I think to myself: there's so much behind it. You can't understand it just like that, because there's a whole process, a whole life behind it. How could you possibly understand?

Why don't you try it? Try to make yourself understood to someone else – your whole being, your contradictions, how you became the person you are, your fears, hopes and desires. Imagine having to do it over and over again, every day.

It's humiliating. Exhausting. Draining.

Perhaps you're religious, and know what it feels like to be asked to explain yourself to someone who rejects spirituality of any kind: that feeling of impossibility.

*

I remember being a teenager and watching talk shows on Islam for the first time. Whenever an imam appeared on them I had to look away, because I couldn't stand watching someone who was highly respected in Muslim communities being displayed, patronised and humiliated. Shows like that speak a secular language, so they would laugh at the imam's language, shaped as it was by religion; shows like that aren't about theology, so they would scoff at his theological arguments; shows like that want to create controversy rather than reach a consensus – so they would respond with disdain to his naive wish to rectify misapprehensions about Islam.

Years later I, too, sat on those stages, and experienced what others had experienced before me – until this happened: a sociology professor, the Chairman of the Council of the Protestant Church in Germany and I had been invited to an on-stage discussion about right-wing populism and tolerance in society. Something about this discussion struck me as unusual: while the professor and

I drew on academic, secular language, the chairman used terms like 'charity' and 'mercy'. It was the first time that I'd heard religious language spoken in such a context without anyone mocking it.

It seemed so abstruse to me that I – the one who, on the basis of the way she dressed, could be easily identified as belonging to a religion – was reluctant to employ religious language, while he spoke it so effortlessly. Admittedly, unlike me, he was a religious functionary; but could I, too, have used religious terms and argued from a religious point of view without anyone questioning my membership of this society, my capacity for rational thought or my intellect? I don't think so.

The experience opened my eyes to how inconsistent society is in its treatment of religion and religious language, and I asked myself a question that may well affect all of us who are religious: what does secular language do to our spirituality? What has it done to me?

*

I first learnt about my religion in Turkish, rather than German, in terms associated with a perspective unknown to the German language. I prayed to God in Turkish, I cried in Turkish, I believed in Turkish. But after 9/11, when I'd just turned thirteen, I was forced to find German words to express this faith, these prayers and thoughts, because other people, German-speaking people, started attacking me about my faith, asking me questions and demanding that I justify myself.

When our innermost being is dragged into the public sphere, when someone feels entitled to scrutinise it, turn it this way and that and pass judgement on it, we become vulnerable in a very particular way. Our feelings – for which we never used to have to find the right words, because they were simply part of us, because prayers are rarely spoken out loud, but rather felt and thought in our hearts – those feelings aren't up to it. Our faith shelters in the vulnerable parts of the heart. Fragile and precious, intimate and personal.

Nobody should force themselves between a believer and God. Yet this is where other people's curious, greedy perspectives inserted themselves.

So I ask myself how anyone can remain spiritual if they constantly have to rationalise, explain and defend their spirituality. In recent years, I have seen one after another of my friends take off her hijab, because – as some of them told me during long, wonderful conversations – they yearned for the faith for which they, as its visible representatives, hardly had any room left.[13] Someone who is religious needs peace and breathing space to feel the love of God – yet they are denied these when they repeatedly have to explain what cannot be explained, in a language that is alien to faith. As the Jewish religious philosopher Martin Buber once wrote, 'The existence of mutuality between God and man cannot be proved, just as God's existence cannot be proved.'[14]

The issue isn't only individual people's curiosity; it's also society's expectations. Our answers to questions about our religion have to be satisfactory in order for our rights not to be curtailed.

What does it do to us, if we have to strip naked so that others can comprehend us – when we then, naked as we are, see ourselves through other people's eyes, to the point that we can no longer recognise ourselves?

It's as if you had to explain to someone to whom love is a foreign concept why you are sharing your life with your partner. You rationalise your love, impose on it a language and way of thinking which you hope will make that person understand – and after numerous failed attempts to explain, you might hear yourself sigh and say something like, 'I live with my partner because they offer me financial security.' Your words thus dissociate themselves from your feelings, and your language from who you are. And you are held captive in the in-between – between language and being.

5

Worthless Knowledge

I don't feel that it is necessary to know exactly what
I am. The main interest in life and work is to become
someone else that you were not in the beginning.

Michel Foucault[1]

In his book *Before You Know It*, the cognitive psychologist
John Bargh investigates how our thinking and behaviour
are subtly shaped by various factors and influences.
For example, how does social identity influence people's
actions and accomplishments? Can someone's social categorisation affect how they behave? He describes a study
by the psychologists Nalini Ambady and Margaret Shih,
who investigated the effects of two widespread cultural
stereotypes in the US: that girls are *bad* at maths, and that
Asians are *good* at maths.

What does this mean for US girls of Asian origin?

Ambady and Shih examined the performance of five-year-old Asian American girls in age-appropriate maths
tests. To do this, they divided them into three groups;
before sitting the test, the girls in the first group were asked
to colour in a picture of two Asian children eating rice with
chopsticks; the girls in group two coloured in a picture of a

girl holding a doll, the girls in group three a neutral landscape. In the maths test, the girls in group one scored above average, the girls in group two below average, and the girls in group three scored average marks.

Bargh describes how the audience gasped when the psychologists presented the results. They not only showed that cultural stereotypes affect performance, but proved that children acquire those stereotypes at the pre-school stage. Toys, TV shows, music, entertainment, everyday interactions between adults, as well as our language all play a part in the early formation of stereotypes that affect our self-image, and therefore our behaviour and ability to succeed. The images they forge are thus rooted in our minds even before we are able to consciously apprehend them. Our self-perception is shaped by other people's distorted perception of us, and defines the horizon of our possibilities, the limits of the self.[2]

*

What images and stereotypes are people exposed to in society? What is your child expected to know? What questions are they expected to be able to answer? With what knowledge do they have to be equipped, to have the right to *be*?

Do they have to be able to explain why their eyes are the shape they are? Do they have to be able to explain the texture and colour of their hair? Do they have to account for the colour of their skin, or why their parents believe what they do, dress as they do and love each other the way they do?

Many don't have to. Children whose skin is creamy or beige and called 'flesh-coloured' – i.e. whose colour is *self-explanatory* – and whose eyes are round – i.e. correspond to the white norm – don't have to explain their parents' relationship or love life. They don't have to know where their parents, grandparents, great-grandparents and great-great-grandparents were born and why they don't 'go back to where they came from'. They don't have to explain why they're *here* instead of somewhere else.

It's the 'other' children, *other people's* children, who don't fit the norm. They have to learn to answer questions like that from a very young age, and their success in society depends on how nice and satisfactory their answers are. So they acquire the necessary knowledge and perfect their responses, which grow more eloquent over time, more inhibiting, more demeaning.

The knowledge they acquire shapes them; it makes them a different person to the one they would have become without those questions. Who would you be today if, ever since you were a child, people had constantly asked you about the reason for the colour of your skin or the texture of your hair? Who would you be, if you answered all their questions, yet people still didn't value you? By comparison, who would you be if this hadn't been your experience? What kinds of adults do children grow up to be, who are asked why the moon is round, why trees grow upwards and whether penguins are birds? People accumulate the knowledge they think they need because otherwise they wouldn't constantly be asked about it. Nevertheless, that kind of knowledge doesn't count as *knowledge*. It is the price we have to pay for being different. We receive no recognition for allowing ourselves to be scrutinised and interrogated, and our attitudes to be tested. Our knowledge is worthless knowledge.

When I'd just turned twenty, I spent a summer in London doing an internship within a – there's no other way to put it – beautiful utopian bubble. I have to call it a utopian bubble, because my experience stands in stark contrast to the racist attacks, oppression and discrimination that were simultaneously happening in the same country, in the same city, probably only minutes away. That summer, I found myself in a workplace with people from different walks of life, religions and parts of the world. When people met me they would ask different questions from the ones I was used to in Germany. 'Why do you wear a hijab?', for example, wasn't part of the small talk. Instead, I was asked what I was studying and what I, Kübra, was interested in – the music I listened to, the films I liked. People were interested in me as a person, not as a representative of Islam. They were interested in me, not in what they projected on to me. It was a liberating but also confusing experience. For me, small talk with non-Muslim strangers in Germany had ultimately always been equivalent to an interrogation about my origins, my faith, my reason, my intelligence, my family, my psyche and my private life. I couldn't conceive that someone who met me who wasn't Muslim might be interested in anything else. I was used to having to reveal, yes, undress myself in a particular way, and didn't know how else to conduct small talk. Now that I was actually allowed to be *myself*, I wondered: who am I? And what am I interested in?

I didn't know the answer. Clumsily, I stumbled into freedom. And enjoyed myself immensely.

*

'Sometimes I sit there and think I'd like to go back home,' says a young Syrian woman, close to tears. I've been invited to give a talk and am sitting in the midst of a diverse group of young women from all over Germany – some of them white Germans, others more or less recent immigrants, others from families that have been here for two or three generations. The young Syrian woman is describing her odyssey through the German education system, since her arrival just under three years ago; how she has, in spite of everything, spent years trying to finish high school in order to finally be able to go to university – and the bureaucratic obstacles, and people too, that have stood in her way. The woman who taught her German had said, 'Not even every German can go to university.' What made her, the 'refugee girl', so special?

Then she lists the questions she's asked about Islam, and about why she doesn't wear a hijab but also doesn't eat pork or drink alcohol. The longer she talks, the more desperate she sounds.

Another young woman in the group fled to Germany from Afghanistan a few years ago. She says that her teacher calls her backward and laughs at her for fasting during Ramadan. She recounts humiliating conversations that end with her merely saying, 'You're right. Yes, you're right.' Then she describes how another student in her class once argued with their teacher about Islam. The next day, an eighteen-year-old boy killed nine people during an attack in Munich, and the teacher was sure that it was the same boy. She told the class that she would call the police. The class protested. When it turned out that the killer was Christian, not Muslim, the teacher said that he must have been mentally ill. 'What if it *had* been my classmate, if it'd been a Muslim refugee – would she also have said that he must be mentally ill?' the young woman asks. 'Are people only allowed to be mentally ill in Europe? What about us, who have witnessed bloodshed, whose parents, siblings or children have been murdered in front of them? And why do they only call *us* terrorists – and not the Americans as well, whose troops are killing people in my country, in Afghanistan? Are their victims not people? Are we animals?'

Her words echo around the room. It's a tough moment.

Then she tells us about her cousins, who have become used to seeing death, for whom a corpse by the roadside is a minor daily occurrence, and about her aunt, who was shot dead on her way to the bakery.

She, too, is close to tears now. I look at these two young women and at their fellow refugees in the room. They're seventeen, eighteen years old at most. Their lives are fundamentally different from those of the other women here. While the latter are busy thinking about starting university and embarking on a new stage in their lives, these girls, who have fled wars, are forced to concern themselves with world politics, racism, discrimination and immigration issues. They didn't choose this, and I can see that they're being turned into people they don't want to be.

They remind me of my teenage years, and of my friendship circle – young refugees and children of immigrants, though I myself have never had to live through a war and am not a refugee. They remind me of how we grew to accept our prescribed roles in society, step by step, encounter by encounter. I was no longer just me, Kübra: I was also a Muslim, and had to answer any question that happened to occur to non-Muslims on the subject of Islam, the wars in Iraq and Afghanistan, terrorism, random quotes from the Quran – I was expected to have an opinion on all of these. I allowed myself to be increasingly robbed of my individuality, willingly answered every question, read up on things and made it my job to inform myself.

One of my first memories of feeling this compulsion happened when I was thirteen. It was shortly after 9/11. I was sitting on the underground with my younger sister, when a middle-aged woman sat down next to us. Having sized us up for some time, she asked whether I wore my hijab voluntarily. 'Yes, of course,' I said. 'No, you don't,' she replied. Then she hectored us about how oppressed we were, and interrogated me about the political situation in Iran, Iraq, Saudi Arabia and elsewhere, countries I'd never been to, countries I didn't know. 'It's nothing to do with me,' I shouted, while she kept going on and on at me. 'That's not my Islam,' I said.

She was still yelling when my sister and I switched to another carriage at the next stop. My heart was pounding like mad. I thought that I had failed. Why wasn't I sufficiently informed about what was going on in those countries? It seemed that, as a Muslim, I had a duty to be, otherwise she wouldn't have interrogated me about it. It was as if I hadn't revised enough for an exam that I should have passed with flying colours.

From then on, I regarded every question I was asked as an assignment. I let complete strangers dictate what I ought to inform myself about, the things I ought to know, merely because of a piece of cloth on my head, merely because of what people projected on to me, my body.

Other people's questions influenced what I learnt about my own religion and pushed my own questions, my own interests, my very own thirst for knowledge into the background. So that I could defend myself, I devoted my time to learning about how the inhuman murders and misdeeds committed by those people in the name of my faith had no actual foundation in my faith – rather than pursuing the religious questions that were actually important to me as an individual, the ones that would help me to grow mentally and emotionally, to build my character, my relationship with nature and with humankind. Things that wouldn't necessarily make me a better defender of, or press officer for, my religion, but a better, kinder, stronger person.

'Don't give in to it, if you don't want to,' I told the young women in the group – about whom I didn't actually really know anything, because we'd been talking exclusively about what others project on to them. 'Perfect strangers don't have the right to know about your stories of flight, your faith, your spirituality or your innermost feelings. Talk about it if you want to, but if you don't want to you don't have to.'

I asked myself: what would I do, think, write and talk

about, what kinds of things would I spend my time on, if there was no hatred, no extremism, no war, no discrimination? What motivates *me*?

I hear only silence.

*

Ironically, battling against other people's distorted views of us can sometimes turn them into a reality; resisting the environment in which we live can itself constitute a kind of assimilation, because resistance can become a habit, making us lose sight of what the actual aims of our resistance were and should be: true freedom, equality and justice.

It isn't only the unlabelled, therefore, who keep the labelled in cages: the labelled sometimes keep themselves caged. By challenging the image forced on them by the labellers, they end up sketching collective counter-portraits; which are perhaps less demonising, more positive, but still monolithic. They fail to make room for the humans caged by the projections: individuals, imperfectly perfect human beings. The collective might now carry a different label, but it remains subject to an act of labelling that is collective and dehumanising.

In 2016, when the Muslim US journalist Noor Tagouri appeared in *Playboy*'s 'Renegades' series – fully clothed and wearing a hijab, and in a self-confident pose that wouldn't have been out of place in *The New York Times* or a Muslim fashion magazine – it sent shockwaves through the Muslim social-media scene. Yet the conversation didn't focus on Noor Tagouri as an individual, or on the interview she gave, but on the fact that a visibly Muslim woman had appeared in *Playboy*. Is *the* Muslim woman allowed to do that?

In an effort to repair the public image of 'Islam', Muslim communities often impose unreasonable expectations on Muslims who appear in the public eye. These expectations are never clearly formulated or explicitly stated, but they're always there. After all – whether they want to or not, whether they explicitly reject the role or not – Muslims who speak in public are treated as spokespeople for *Islam* as a whole.

When almost two billion people are reduced to a homogeneous mass, it's only a matter of time before they start obsessing about their media image. If a reductive portrait of them is going to be painted, they want to know exactly by whom and how they are going to be represented: without a hijab, with a hijab, tied this way or that, with a beard, without a beard, representing the standpoint of this or that nation, according to this or that Muslim school of thought, Shiite or Sunni, Wahhabi or Sufi, cultural or practising, liberal or conservative?

Young women experience an even greater pressure of representation, especially when they wear the hijab. Everyone appears to think they are qualified to assess and judge them. If a woman ties the hijab under her chin, she's a conservative; if she drapes it around her head like a turban, she's a progressive; if she wears skirts, she belongs to this community, if she wears tight trousers, to that one. Whether she stops wearing her hijab, or has never worn one – whatever she does or wears, in whatever manner she exists, she is scrutinised, judged and condemned, cat-egorised, catalogued, robbed of her multifacetedness and dehumanised – not only by the society that wants to make her intelligible, but also by the Muslim communities who expect her to explain and 'appropriately' represent Islam. It's an impossible task.

In 2013, a two-minute fashion video entitled 'Some-where in America #MIPSTERZ' was uploaded to the internet, in which young Muslim women are seen celebrat-ing their fashion-conscious, pop-culture lifestyle. Young women on skateboards, laughing and dancing – for weeks, the video was discussed on social media, frame by frame. Is *the* Muslim woman allowed to dress like that, and to move like that, to that kind of music?

I think that, in such cases, some of the reasons behind the criticism are legitimate and important, for example when it comes to the sexism of magazines like *Playboy*; or to the diversification of models in fashion campaigns, which isn't motivated by a desire for inclusiveness, but by the discovery of the buying-power of non-Western, or non-white, consumers – while in Bangladesh and elsewhere, those who produce the very same clothes that are being advertised continue to be appallingly exploited, which thus makes diversity in advertising nothing but a fig leaf. But the critics often aren't in the least interested in political or ethical issues. Instead, piece by piece, we Muslims take away the space that we – and especially Muslim women – need to express our individuality, and our freedom to grow, evolve and make mistakes. The pressure to act in an 'exemplary' manner at all times, to be flawless, pervades our everyday lives and takes away our humanity – after all, it is our flaws and quirks that make us human.

At the same time, this insistence on flawlessness prevents us from talking about appalling misconduct, for example when prominent male clerics abuse their power to hush up sexual violence and intimidate female members of their congregation; it nips any frank discussion of such abuse in the bud, and whoever does try to talk about it is scorned as a 'feminazi', as Westernised or disloyal.[3]

Another example of the obsession that can arise in response to a particular group's public image is the establishment of the 'strong Black woman' stereotype in the US, which portrays Black women as inherently strong, resigned, resilient and self-reliant, especially in films and other popular culture. Studies have shown that this supposedly positive image can prevent healthy stress-management and aggravate depression.[4] What is striking in this context is that a considerable number of medical personnel in the US believe that Black people have a higher pain threshold, which affects the provision of medical treatment.[5] The writer and actor Robin Thede tackled the subject in a satirical music video, in which she raps about 'weak Black women' and criticises the excessive, and dehumanising, expectations imposed on Black women.[6]

In his collection *Desintegriert euch!* ('Deintegrate yourselves!'), the lyrical poet Max Czollek calls on us to 'get away from this idea of identity groups, from this idea that we are whole and need to defend our wholeness'. He argues that each of us is made of many parts, which keep shifting around; to believe that there is such a thing as a 'unified identity' is a 'dangerous illusion'.[7] In this, Czollek draws among other things on a famous line by the Armenian-Turkish journalist Hrant Dink: 'When you can only maintain your identity through an enemy image, your identity is a disease.'[8]

This is why we mustn't let *yet another* generation of young people be reduced to spokespersons for the category to which they supposedly belong; it is why we mustn't raise *yet another* generation who consider it their duty to be the flawless representatives of their group, always ready to argue for their right to exist and to satisfy the public's seemingly insatiable appetite for more and more controversy.

*

When I raised the issue of representation on Instagram, a slam poet replied:

> I always feel that, as a person from an immigrant background, I have to begin by explaining everything, why I'm here, and why I have the right to be here. Do you feel that pressure too? It's like I'm in a creative vicious circle now, because I feel that I'm always expected to talk about these topics (antiracism, the migrant experience, etc.).

To claim individuality and live it doesn't imply a lack of solidarity. Quite the opposite: it's about paving the way for other marginalised people, so that they, too, can tell their individual stories; it's about going through life pursuing your dreams in such a way that discriminating structures are contested rather than reinforced and made manifest, seemingly unshakable and irrevocable. A woman heading up a company won't automatically create greater gender equality; but someone who heads up a company and fights against unfair and sexist structures probably will.

I sometimes manage to do justice to my own resolutions, yet sometimes I fail too, whether because I'm not up to it, or because I'm not paying enough attention, or simply because I don't have the strength or the energy. It isn't easy. When you set out on a new path, you don't know where it'll lead – the dangers that lurk there, how to prepare for them and what groundwork to lay. That's why mistakes are inevitable. But the goal is key: not letting injustice dictate your life, while simultaneously showing solidarity with those not privileged enough to escape it.

*

In 2017, Germany's AfD (Alternative für Deutschland) party won 12.6 per cent of the votes in the general election, and for the first time since the formation of the Federal Republic of Germany a right-wing, openly racist party was sitting in parliament.[9] I wrote an article at the time that begins a few days before the election:

> My heart was pounding. My chest felt tight. A feeling of dread rose inside me. Summer was over. After weeks of travel, I'd finally landed in Hamburg again. At the airport, we got on the train. I carefully tried to read

the faces of the people around us. Were they friendly or hostile? What were they thinking right now, about me, my husband and our child?

Minutes earlier, when we queued at passport control, we were greeted by an official who pointed at us and almost yelled, 'Anyone without a German passport, stand over there!' Again and again he strode among the queues, and in the end simply shouted, 'Turks over there! Turks over there!' He glared at us, but we stayed put, holding our German passports. He continued making his way through the queues, gesticulating wildly with his arms, as if it wasn't people standing there, but bothersome flies that he had to swat away.

Now, on the train, people were looking at us differently to the way they did abroad. Some were looking at us disparagingly, others were sneering. I looked over at my little boy, who was just openly watching those around him, seeking eye contact. Some responded, but many ignored him.

I was uncomfortable. Here, in the city where I was born, in my 'home town'.

I looked at my husband, wondering whether he felt the same. Was I being overly sensitive? Most people can't tell where he's from or what his religion is just by looking at him. The society he experiences when we are out and about together is different to the one he experiences when he's on his own.

Finally I whispered, 'I feel uncomfortable.' He leant towards me and said, 'Me too.' I was relieved.

Relieved to know that it wasn't me, that I wasn't being 'oversensitive'.

Yet nothing out of the ordinary happened that day. Nobody swore or yelled at me, and if I hadn't just come back from weeks spent travelling around the world it would have been a completely normal day. It is only contrasting experiences that make you feel the strain, and make it unbearable – the strain that I quickly got used to again in the days that followed – because unease has become part of our lives, our being.

A few weeks later, I was sitting in front of the TV with the editors of a major German weekly, to analyse the election results. When they were announced, Alexander Gauland, the AfD's lead candidate, said, 'We'll hunt her [Merkel] down.' He said that the government should dress up warm, and that 'we'll get our people back'.[10]

A shiver ran down my spine. I was ready for anything, but not for the force, the chill of those words. Afterwards, as I walked along the streets, I wondered who among those around me had voted for this party, with its policy of hate towards marginalised groups and minorities. I wondered who among the people walking past me had voted against the right of people like me to belong here.

A day passed. Two days. My eyes stopped looking for answers. I'd grown used to the cold.

Then I came across these words from the philosopher Rabbi Abraham Joshua Heschel: 'I would say about individuals, an individual dies when he ceases to be surprised. I am surprised every morning that I see the sunshine again. When I see an act of evil, I am not accommodated. I don't accommodate myself to the violence that goes on everywhere; I'm still surprised. That's why I'm against it, why I can hope against it. We must learn how to be surprised, not to adjust ourselves. I am the most maladjusted person in society.'[11]

His words made me think of the saying – sometimes attributed to the Indian philosopher Jiddu Krishnamurti – that 'it is no measure of health to be well adjusted to a profoundly sick society'.

I don't know how it's done: how you can never cease to be surprised, never get used to injustice, keep showing your solidarity and remain watchful – and yet live your life, rejoice in life and go your own way.

But I think that the moment we make this our aim the way will start paving itself. The moment we become aware of the images that influence us, and decide not to submit to their influence, the way will start paving itself. The moment we become aware of our dehumanisation and resolve to make room for our individuality without being invited or given permission to do so – and without ceasing to stand in solidarity with others – the way will start paving itself.

6

The Intellectual Cleaning Lady

The best way to know about a problem is to be part of it.

Anand Giridharadas, Winners Take All[1]

I've been a part of many problems in my life, and have made many mistakes with the best of intentions. Particularly mistakes that, in the context of a liberal-capitalist society, are not considered mistakes but desirable, rational behaviour.

I was once at a dinner with feminist women when a white woman who was slightly younger than me, and like me a public figure, made me think of my younger self, and of how uncomfortable I had felt back then. In that moment, I thought I'd met someone who shared this feeling, so I asked her if she was familiar with the discomfort that comes with being given the power to speak into a microphone on behalf of so many people.

When I was in my early twenties, a public broadcaster invited me to a TV debate. The title was nicely lurid – a pinch of Islam here, a pinch of imaginary German 'core culture' there. I should have turned it down, but back then I really believed that I would be able to help discredit some of the prevailing prejudices, and it didn't occur to me that

I was in fact participating in a business model called 'fear of Islam'. The other guests on the list looked OK; only one among them promised tension. He's a habitual talk-show attendee nowadays, but at the time he wasn't very well known yet. Up to that point, his contribution to such shows had consisted mainly of confirming other people's fears or concerns about 'Islam', and it was for this reason that most of my friends advised me not to go. 'It's not worth arguing with him,' they said. Only one of them disagreed. He was the only one who had met him personally, having interviewed him recently, and he thought that he was definitely someone with whom you could have a proper discussion. I thought it sounded all right. After all, he didn't have to agree with me, so long as he was interested in a genuine exchange of views. I had what I thought was a sound plan: I would meet him for a coffee beforehand, and if he really was interested in the subject we'd be able to enrich the show with our discussion. So long as it remained constructive, it wouldn't matter if things got heated.

So far, so naive. We met before the show, and I found him to be extremely pleasant to talk to. We talked about the German Muslim community's problems, but also criticised Islamophobia and racism.[2] I thought we got on well – until we were sitting in the studio with the cameras rolling.

Prompted by a question from the host, I started talking about Islamophobia. The man who just now had been so calm and thoughtful brusquely interjected that it wasn't an issue. Surprised, I explained that Islamophobia *is* an issue.

'Islamophobia sounds like a disease,' he replied. 'Are you saying that the Germans are sick?'

I stared at him, stunned. How do you react to someone who becomes a completely different person when the cameras are rolling? The audience behind me cheered, but the host didn't intervene. From then on, the audience heckled me whenever I started talking. At one point I turned to the audience, outraged; when the show was broadcast later, you couldn't see or hear any of this.

After the show, I still couldn't quite understand what had happened. I went up to him and raised the subject of his comparing Islamophobia to a disease. He said he'd merely meant to be polemical and disruptive. I asked what he thought his comment would achieve. 'Well,' he said, nodding, 'maybe it was a mistake.' He turned round and helped himself to the buffet.

Later, my friends told me that 'the programme was OK, really'. They said it was normal for people to act differently when they're on camera. But for me, such hardened unscrupulousness goes against the grain: how can someone be deliberately polemical, even intentionally say something that they know to be wrong, on a sensitive subject? Didn't he know that words have consequences?

This man was someone who 'explained' Islam to the German public by confirming their fears, while I was trying to take away their fear. As it turns out, however, we were essentially playing the same role, only from opposite ends of the stage: we were both being forced to speak for all Muslims. We were both explaining to an audience of unlabelled people what was hiding behind the glass wall

While he was spreading panic, I was calming things down, but both of us were keeping the cage alive.

Who had assigned this role to me? I, too, could have spread fear for the sake of applause and recognition. No one in this media circus had verified that I was genuine, so no one could have stopped me from abusing the authority I'd been granted.

That's what I was thinking of when I asked the young woman about the discomfort that comes with being in a position of power. She replied that it was typical for a woman to ask such a question – an old white man never would. She was right: no one who considers their authority unassailable would ask themselves such a question. But I know that I have my limitations. I know my *acziyet*.

One of the mistakes I've made is that I have spent years playing the game – that game of attaching collective labels to people. It was the job of my antagonists to reinforce collective definitions from the standpoint of an insider, and my job to speak on behalf of those who are fighting against those labels. The question that the public was asking us was: which of you is right? As if one side were lying, while the other was in possession of the absolute truth. But there is no such thing as the absolute truth. Yes, there are women who are forced to wear a hijab. Yes, there are women who wear the hijab voluntarily. Yes, there are Muslims who fight against terrorism. Yes, there are Muslims who commit _____ _____. Yes, the overwhelming majority of terror-
_____ Yes, the overwhelming majority of men are
____. The question is, what do we regard as the
___ what do we regard as the norm?

The Intellectual Cleaning Lady

The battle for absolute truth is good business. Nowadays, you can make a living from being a critic of Islam. Yet it makes no sense to fight over trite, conclusive truths concerning an entire group of people. As a society, we are stagnating. The problems, meanwhile, persist.

So I sat in those studios, saying, 'Yes, but ...' I tried to explain the reasons behind the problems we were facing and to turn stigmatising discussions into constructive ones. I was like an intellectual janitor, pointlessly sweeping up the bullshit people left behind and countering it with numbers, data, facts and common sense. I have spent a large part of my adult life performing damage limitation, always ready to counter the next racist idiocy being sold to us as intellectual debate or 'legitimate criticism of Islam'.

Regardless of what our day job might be, women who are feminists or environmental activists, especially women of colour, who speak out in public are expected to be ready to put aside everything else – their private lives, their work – and to step into the breach at a moment's notice. Take Laura Dornheim, for example, who is a manager at a software company as well as a German Green Party activist: she, too, is one of those people who are expected to drop everything for the sake of their cause and are exposed to attacks on social media which sometimes cross over into the physical world. During a particularly difficult time, she wrote me this:

> I want to scream 'What do you want from me?' into the darkness, the tangible darkness of anonymity – from which someone is currently sending daily deliveries of

luxury goods worth hundreds of euros to my home address, on account. What do they want from me?

I know exactly what they want, of course. They think they can force their superiority down my throat and publicly humiliate me, just to promote their own sick egos. They're probably hoping to silence politically active women, and think they can force me to engage with them.

Sadly, the latter is true. As much as I hate them for it, and though I actually had better things to do tonight, I'm almost obsessively refreshing my mentions every few seconds to see if anything new comes up.

It's a physical experience. Anyone who has experienced violence, analog or digital, will know the feeling. My pupils become dilated, and at the same time I get total tunnel vision. My pulse quickens and I almost feel faint. I feel sick. My body is scared. I'm scared. True, it's only a few tweets, only a few errant parcels. For now.

I know that I won't let anyone keep me from speaking out about the things I believe in. But it's a high price that I and so many others have to pay, and keep paying.

And I know that, for many, the price is far too high.

This cost of being in the public eye is often trivialised, and thus normalised. We are put under pressure to respond, to make ourselves available.

When I asked a number of women in the public eye about this, the journalist Anna Dushime replied,

Firstly, I feel guilty towards my community if I don't say something and make use of my (still comparatively small) platform. Secondly, it makes me angry when insensitive white friends do things like send me a video showing police violence, along the lines of, 'Isn't it awful, what happened in St Louis? Have you seen this?' I always wonder why they prioritise their desire for an authentic reaction from a Black person over my well-being. Thirdly, I get upset when people in my professional world expect me to pretty much hold a press conference, ideally followed by a workshop. But I don't owe them a learning experience. So I have to sort out those feelings, while at the same time trying to digest the racist or sexist event they're alluding to.

The journalist Vanessa Vu commented:

Situations in which you feel helpless, triggered for example by racist, sexist or classist aggression, are like accidents: I can't and don't want to look away, I stop in my tracks and want to make things better – and while I'm doing that, I'm neglecting my own needs and goals. Once or twice is OK, but, unlike accidents, I'm confronted with racist incidents every day. That constant first-aid effort takes up a huge amount of energy and intellectual capacity, which I'd rather invest in innovative, empowering and lasting work.

For many years now, the feminist author Margarete Stokowski has worked on this precise interface with her popular and widely shared column, in which, in her professional guise, she critically analyses political, social and cultural occurrences; meanwhile, as a private individual, she is increasingly becoming something of a projection screen for people with racist and sexist attitudes. She once told me about the expectations levied on her:

> I think it's a learning process that anyone who is politically active has to go through: realising that you have to be aware of your own limits, because other people usually aren't – and even when they are, it makes sense to know your own abilities and needs, and act accordingly. As important as the cause you're fighting for is, it's just as important to look after your health and ability to do your job – and I can understand how people can suffer from 'activist burnout'. Personally, I don't feel that I always have to say something, even when others ask me to. For me, being free not to comment on everything or instantly have an opinion ready on every subject is much more important than the need to respond to or take a position on everything. It's harder when others are being attacked. I find it harder to stay quiet then, and try to help in some way, even if I don't actually have the resources for it (time, energy, willpower, etc.). Sometimes it's exhausting, but I don't think it should change either.

For years, the London-based French-Irish journalist and film-maker Myriam François kept being invited – as an openly Muslim, feminist woman – to engage with extreme views on talk shows and panel discussions. Yet she told me that they are devised in such a way that the participants sometimes find themselves arguing for positions that they don't actually agree with, and as a result sometimes even involuntarily increase division. She no longer takes part in such discussions. 'I'm not a circus animal. I'm not here to entertain you. I understand that that's how TV works, but personally I'm not interested.' In an interview with Nesrine Malik, the journalist and author Otegha Uwagba expresses similar thoughts when reflecting on her past work: 'I'm thirty years old now, I've spent my entire life treading around white people's feelings.' But Uwagba highlights that now, with her 2020 book *Whites: On Race and Other Falsehoods*, 'I want them to feel uncomfortable. I want them to feel challenged. I want them to feel confronted.'[3]

I, too, came to realise that those who orchestrate these exhibition bouts rely on the fact that people like François, Uwagba and me will fight our corner, and that the show only works because we join in.

Our reactions, even our outrage can turn into an integral part of the game. In her article 'Why I'm no longer giving racist marketing campaigns my outrage', the journalist Paula Akpan wonders if outrage is in fact actively provoked by brands: 'Is it truly inconceivable to some that these marketing teams may actually be doing it on purpose? What has become abundantly clear is that Black rage is free publicity. [...] The cycle seems to consist of the following: brand displays offensive material, online community responds with anger, disbelief and calls for boycott of brand, brand takes down offensive material and releases vapid statement using phrases like "we deeply regret", "does not reflect our core beliefs" and "we are committed to representing diversity", rage cools off, calls for boycotts are forgotten, business as usual for the brand.' To Akpan, this is not about ignoring racist ads and campaigns, but reflecting critically about how to react – and 'acknowledging that these are deliberate and calculated marketing ploys, where such online buzz will have these companies trending worldwide'.[4]

Editors are neglecting their journalistic duty of care when they task us – the targeted, marginalised, attacked and mocked – with countering their guests' false, knowingly provocative and deliberately xenophobic, racist and discriminatory statements. These past years, I've spent a lot of time explaining to editors that it's *their* responsibility to unmask their guests' mistakes, lies, manipulations and provocations – not mine. Outsourcing what is a journalist's essential duty lends xenophobia, racism, sexism, etc. the status of an *opinion* or *position* – which then makes our contribution merely a *counter-opinion* or *counter-position*.

Far too many editors and publishers shy away from taking responsibility for their work, because they think that discussions that negotiate someone's right to exist are seemingly *just* discussions. Just words. Just a game. But a word is never just a word. Every word has an effect. People change because of the words we use to describe them – they become what is ascribed to them.

In his book *Whistling Vivaldi*, the psychologist Claude

Steele describes how social stereotypes influence those whom they portray. He discovered that the fear of corresponding to a negative stereotype can result in that very stereotype becoming reality, arguing that our social identity affects our performance at school, our powers of recall, the extent to which we need to prove ourselves, and how relaxed we feel in certain environments. All these are things which we generally assume are determined by individual talent, level of ambition and personality.

Steele and his colleagues demonstrate that merely *being conscious* of negative assumptions about your social group affects individual performance – even when our being part of this or that group is supposedly irrelevant in the context of the test environment. There is no need for there to be someone actually in the room who agrees with the stereotype; it affects us simply because it exists in society, and because those affected by it know that it exists.[5]

*

I had only been a full-time writer for a few years when I came across this quote from Nietzsche: 'Whoever lives for the sake of combating an enemy has an interest in the enemy's staying alive.'[6] I wondered whether, somewhere deep down inside me, I had become dependent on this destructive mechanism, whereby people produce hate-filled discourse while others react to it. Could it be that I actually – somewhere deep down – wanted to maintain the systems I was struggling against? I realised with relief that I didn't. But I also realised that many of my life decisions still orientated themselves around it. I decided to stop earning a living as a journalist for a few years, and instead worked at a university. I wanted to put my motives to the test, to uncouple my value as a person from the public, official recognition I had gained.

I realised that I didn't miss any of it. Instead, I felt light, free. My work had nothing to do with current political developments; its reach was more limited. One day, an old friend of mine (white, male) who works in the media told me that he had bad news for me: he believed that Islam and immigration would no longer be the most important topics in public discourse in the future. 'That's the bad news?' I asked him, laughing. I couldn't think of anything more wonderful than no longer having to play the part of the scapegoat for socio-political crises. I couldn't think of anything more wonderful than no longer having to be part of a game that merely distracts us from the real problems.

Toni Morrison once said, 'The function, the very serious function of racism [...] is distraction. It keeps you from doing your work. It keeps you explaining, over and over again, your reason for being. Somebody says you have no language and so you spend twenty years proving that you do. Somebody says your head isn't shaped properly so you have scientists working on the fact that it is. [...] None of that is necessary. There will always be one more thing.'[7]

There will always be something else. Another absurdity, another 'expert opinion' on which I and thousands of others expend our lives, instead of dedicating ourselves to interesting and forward-looking topics. We are wasting our energy fighting a pointless battle, to simply make sure that things don't get worse.

A few years ago I was in the audience at a panel discussion which included a highly regarded journalist. He joked around, saying that Muslims are so easily roused because they don't get enough sex or alcohol. Then, in all seriousness, he asked his fellow panellists whether there was a link between Islam and a refusal to be educated. I stared at him from my seat in the audience. Our eyes met. He obviously hadn't expected *my kind* among the audience that evening. So he avoided my eyes. I got up to say something and he turned away. 'Aren't you allowed to look at me? Or does my existence puzzle you?' I asked. Clearly that was the case: after all, if what he'd suggested was true, women like me couldn't possibly exist. When I approached him after the event and asked where his views came from, he said, 'I'm no expert on Islam. They just invite me to these things, and it's good when there's a bit of a hoo-ha.'

When she was a child, Maya Angelou didn't speak for five years. She was eight when she named a friend of her mother's as the man who raped her. Shortly later, he was found dead. It was then that she stopped talking, afraid of the power of her words.[8]

A child believes, to the point of error, in the power of her words, while a grown man thinks he can say anything just for fun. Put another way, an innocent eight-year-old girl takes responsibility for her words, while adults deliberately spread messages of hate to cause 'a bit of a hoo-ha'. But the more polarised such exhibition fights are, the more they change the audience they want to entertain. The more unequivocal and homogenous the positions, the more idealised and uncompromising the attitudes, the deeper the social chasm becomes. There's barely room for doubt, hesitation or reflection; and in the end we forget that they were ever possible.

'I should be allowed to say ...': in media discourses, that phrase puts decency, respect and empathy, as well as scholarship and facts, on the back foot. We saw it during the Trump presidency, when there was a vast shift in political discourse in terms of what was considered acceptable for politicians, including presidents, to say. In the US, Trump used sexist, racist and otherwise deroga-tory language in relation to refugees, religious minorities and immigrants, and insisted on using the term 'China virus' when talking about Covid-19 – despite experts' warnings of anti-Asian hate crimes.[9] In the UK in 2018, the then-MP Boris Johnson, who as a journalist had called Black people 'picaninnies' and gay men 'tank-topped bumboys', compared Muslim women who wear the niqab to 'letterboxes',[10] and Islamophobic attacks rose by 375 per cent.[11] And in Germany this was perfectly exemplified by the politician Thilo Sarrazin, whose 2010 book (the third-bestselling title in Germany since the war, after the *Duden* – the German equivalent of the *Oxford English Dictionary* – and the Bible),[12] as well as various statements on Turkish and Arab immigrants allegedly conquering Germany with their higher birth rates, incited a decade of racist public debate. The author Hatice Akyün describes the event as a rupture:

Thilo Sarrazin permanently shifted the limits of what you can say. Media editors fed their readership statements that would normally be a case for prosecution. We were now talking casually and urbanely about eugenics, putrid racism, and whether immigrants are an asset to Germany. A crass counting-house bureaucrat's dubious clichés were for ever being repeated as if they had a foundation in science. Behind the façade of the law-abiding citizen to whom the media gave a solid platform, followers were becoming radicalised and seeing themselves as the official executors of crude categorisations, shallowness and biased blame-games.

Akyün says that her colleagues argued that not everything Sarrazin said was wrong – 'and then they rooted around in the swamp of words for that one drop of clear water'.[13]

Similarly, the columnist Jennifer Rubin criticised her fellow colleagues and the media's failure to decode Trump's racist and sexist comments. 'It allows the Republican attack machine to escape accountability,' Rubin wrote.[14] Instead of simply *reporting on* and hence reproducing Trump's derogatory and discriminatory attacks, often directed at women of colour, the media should *contextualise* and *decode* his insults. As Rubin says, it is important to explain that 'these are common insults Trump throws at women, meant to deprive them of respect, status and power. It is meant to reinforce the stereotype that women must be docile, respectful and pleasing to men. The put-downs are especially egregious in connection with women of color, who for decades were relegated to domestic and service jobs and expected to be non-confrontational. In short, spell it out. This is a moment for education, insight and accountability in which the media must play their part.'

If the media does not decode, debunk, expose and unmask politicians' hateful rhetoric, it will degenerate into the mere plaything of demagogues. Editors will turn into spectators voyeuristically drooling over the next 'inappropriate' moment until the inappropriate sets the norm. Until the inappropriate is the new normal. Until it's too late.

*

A problem doesn't usually just show up suddenly, but takes years to come to the fore. Some – those at the margins, the less privileged – see the lines it draws through society; but those lines often turn up in places that privileged people don't visit, which is why they only notice the problem when it affects them directly. The warnings of the marginalised, the less privileged, go unheard. Their experience, their knowledge, their insights are deemed unimportant, irrelevant to society at large.

But later may be too late. Even if the privileged have no selfless interest in, or sympathy for, the less privileged – if they want to know what might lie in store for them, they should at least take a look at what those 'others' are experiencing. If you want to know the challenges that await us all, you should listen closely to those who are already suffering under the current social structures. The poor around the world, the marginalised around the world – they have

seen the ugly face of the climate crisis, capitalism, con-
sumerism and social media. It's sometimes both funny and
tragic, watching the privileged as they try to figure out the
challenges of the future, while ignoring the people who are
already facing those challenges and have long spoken and
written about them.

By the time the privileged realise that right-wing populism and right-wing extremism are a serious threat to
democracy, the victims of right-wing attitudes will have
been warning about it for years. This is true for any threat
from fascism and intolerance, however embedded in politics it is or how laughably invalid it may seem: whether
it's UKIP or Trump, English Defence League marches or
the storming of the Capitol, if you are able to ignore it,
that says a lot about you and your privilege. That's why
we, as a society, can't afford to ignore hatred. We have to
put xenophobia in its place, instead of tolerating it and
raising it to the status of an 'opinion' bringing a fresh
perspective to the table. We have to call it by its name:
racism. Extremism. Xenophobia. Fascism. Hate is *not* an
opinion.

For the majority of people, racist, xenophobic and discriminatory debates only become real when there are mobs
chasing people, setting buildings on fire or committing
murder. The majority only notice hate, viciousness, violence, rejection – daily realities for people like me, people
marked out as 'different' – when things escalate dramatically. The experiences of minorities and marginalised
groups are portents. We should listen closely when they
describe what happens in the shadows – for which there

are sometimes no words. They are the seismograph that registers threats to our democracy.

The author Mely Kiyak talked about this phenomenon in her 2016 Otto Brenner Prize acceptance speech, describing the vicious comments levelled at journalists of colour or from immigrant backgrounds:

> Ever since my first article – a lead feature in the *Zeit*'s 'Arts and Culture' section on 19 January 2006 – there hasn't been a single piece, not a single column or interview, which didn't prompt the kind of reaction I've just described [hate comments and hate letters]. Not a single one! Whereas some of my colleagues have received maybe three letters in their entire career!
>
> Incidentally, I'm not talking about online comments, but actual letters and emails. Week in and week out, outrage, insults, complaints and threats hail down on me. Few have anything to do with what I have written; they're mostly about the fact that I've written at all.
>
> So I can't take it seriously when people quote some study or other showing that readers are more aggressive these days because of Facebook and Twitter. In my experience, things have always been this way.
>
> Ten years ago, whenever we – a handful of colleagues with names that sound a bit different – told our colleagues that we were being seriously harassed and asked them to show their support, the reaction was always the same: indifference, and the mistaken belief that what was happening was a problem affecting only

a minority of people. Despite the fact that we told them, 'Today it's us, tomorrow it'll be you!'

But the experiences of the few have to matter, because they keep turning out to be indicators of what's to come.

It took ten years for our colleagues to acknowledge hate speech as a problem, and to write about it. The crazy thing is, they say, 'It wasn't as bad then as it is now. These days, everything's more crude and uninhibited.'

It isn't true, of course. It was just as bad, despicable, obscene and primitive back then. Yet it only affected 'us'.[15]

Digital hate speech has created dismay and widespread discussion in recent years, but for some people it long constituted the background noise for their public work. In 2016, the author Anne Wizorek and I asked other feminists, 'What is online hate speech doing to you?' At the time, Wizorek wrote that it had taken away our peace of mind, our 'light-heartedness'. The management consultant Dudu Küçükgöl wrote that it consumes too much of our 'time and energy'; Margarete Stokowski said she was 'tired, exhausted'; and the politician Amina Yousaf replied, 'Before every post, I think about whether I can write/share/post it without being scared. I've started censoring myself.' In 'How to be a woman online', the feminist and writer Laura Bates writes: 'The problem with being a woman on the internet isn't just the abuse. It's the crushing weight of all the people who want to tell you how to deal with it.'[16]

And the journalist Ash Sarkar writes about the consequences of the abuse she experienced online following an Islamophobic tweet by a columnist, saying that it 'severely affected my mental health. I couldn't sleep, and had bouts of trembling and heart palpitations. [...] The unfortunate truth is that, sometimes, the only thing that separates an anonymous troll and a journalist is a byline. [...] Those at the top of our industry have persistently drawn a veil of silence around the bullying tactics that drum black and brown women out of public life. We cannot claim to have a truly free press as long as those who tacitly encourage and facilitate the harassment of women of colour remain sheltered within the media.'[17]

You don't have to take part in political discourse to experience that hatred. Some people are a target simply because they are visible online; thus Black people, people of colour, people who identify as LGBTQ+, people with a disability and women are frequently at the receiving end.

Whenever we raised the issue of online hate speech, the usual response was that we shouldn't make such a fuss, because it's 'just' the internet; or that if you speak out in public you have to expect some negative reaction. People claimed that the problem wasn't hate, it was us, that we must have 'provoked' it. That was before the debate about online hate speech reached white, male editors – before it became part of privileged people's reality.

The debate thus keeps changing according to whatever happens to be trending. Xenophobic, sexist and racist points of view continue to be elevated to the status of an opinion, and we're expected to respond to them. We're invited to step into the arena, and then asked to sweep up, explain, defend. We're supposed to play a game that relies on the dehumanisation of people. How much longer can we – do we *want* to – do this?

*

We begged you to stop amplifying and normalising hatred and racism. But you told us we were 'politically correct' and 'freedom of speech' was more important. The more you gave the far right a platform, the more powerful they got. We begged you.

Osman Faruqi[18]

We live in strange times. When you suffer, you're not meant to wear your suffering on your sleeve but to swallow it, hide it, so that other people will accept you and see the human being inside you. Even now, we think that someone is 'brave' when they talk about their depression – but only if they don't demand structural change, and *take charge of their fate*. People who enjoy a privileged life shouldn't be burdened with things that keep others from doing the same, such as poverty, existential angst, deep anxiety or paralysing pain. If you don't have a care in the world, you shouldn't have other points of view forced on you, or, worse, be forced to question your own happiness.

Some people thus learn to conceal the fact that they have a hard life, and affect light-heartedness. For example, people like the elderly gentleman who lived in our old neighbourhood, who knew better than to talk too much, to ask for help too often or put other people out more than necessary, who was worried that he would become a burden. I wasn't able to take that fear away from him at the time. Sometimes, when we invited him over to ours for a party, I would notice that he – who had a treasure trove of stories to tell – suppressed a desire to join in; in order not to be rejected by those younger and quicker than him, he would just nod silently and – unlike anyone else in the room – never talk about his own life or experiences, never complain or share his troubles with us. The illusion of belonging.

It's similar with racist experiences in our society. Someone who is harassed, jostled, disparaged or glared at with loathing every day gradually learns that it's better not to complain – be it to your colleagues, your fellow students or your friends at the gym, to whom these things don't happen. They learn not to shatter other people's illusion that everything's well with the world, and to hide the indignities they suffer. But they're real. For me, racism is part of everyday life. Since I've become a mother, I've even been physically attacked several times. In June 2015, a Muslim woman's hijab was ripped off in London;[19] in September 2016, a man was arrested after a racist attack on a pregnant Muslim woman in London that caused her to miscarry;[20] and in March 2019, a pregnant woman in Berlin was punched in the stomach by a man – the incident report said that she'd been attacked because of her hijab, but it wasn't her hijab that caused the attack, it was the fact that the attacker was a racist.[21] For the other people who are – in a symbolic and political sense – simultaneously being targeted in racist attacks like these, such incidents aren't abstract numbers or statistics. They pay careful attention to how the dominant society reacts: whose family is visited? Outside which buildings do they post guards to deter would-be attackers? Do lots of people change their profile pictures on Facebook, Twitter and Instagram? Do they offer their condolences? What is being discussed in special programmes and talk shows?

When a politician, such as the UK MP Jo Cox in 2016 or the German politician Walter Lübcke in 2019, is murdered, it's irrelevant whether or not the murder turns out to be politically motivated. As long as there's the mere suspicion that it might be, the question is: how do we deal with it? Anyone at whom the murder may have been directed will closely watch the reaction of the media and politicians, and ask themselves: whose threats and fears are being prioritised, what are they looking at with particular interest, and at what point will there be an almost hyperbolic call for 'mindfulness' and restraint?

Remember 15 March 2019, when a right-wing terrorist strapped a camera to his head and live-streamed a killing spree in which he murdered fifty people in two mosques in Christchurch, New Zealand? In the days that followed, the most widely watched political talk shows on German TV were on the following topics: 'From peak performance to overload: When your job can make you ill', 'Women under pressure, men in charge: Has anything changed?' and 'Anti-European populists: Is Brexit just the beginning?' And so the people at whom the murders were directed wonder: do our lives merit empathy?

However, what matters is not only *whether* a terrorist attack is covered, but *how*. Research has shown that New Zealand and Australian media coverage of the Christchurch mosque attack 'exhibited significant disparity in editorial decision-making'.[22] Gavin Ellis and Denis Miller conducted interviews and analysed hundreds of news pieces, and discovered that

> New Zealand media were focused largely on empathetic coverage of victims and resisted the alleged gunman's attempts to publicise his cause while their Australian counterparts showed no such reluctance and ran extended coverage of the alleged perpetrator, along with material ruled objectionable in New Zealand. [...] The editorial focus in each case exhibits the effect of proximity, identified in literature on empirical ethical decision-making as a factor in applied ethicality. [...] A proximity filter was used by New Zealand media who identified the victims as part of their own community, but the events of 15 March 2019 were seen as 'foreign' by Australian journalists who used perceived distance as justification for extremely graphic content.

In the UK, the *Daily Mirror* described the terrorist attacker as an 'angelic boy who former associates revealed was a likeable and dedicated personal trainer running free athletic programmes for kids'.[23] Houssem Ben Lazreg, who also analysed media coverage of the massacre, writes that 'when white individuals commit horrendous acts, it seems news outlets portray them as people deserving of humanity. They are portrayed with complicated personalities: the little "angel" who went astray even after being revealed as a vicious and violent racist'.[24] Again, we're forced to ask who gets to be a complicated individual – who gets to be seen as angelic, as innocent even when guilty, and who is viewed as always somehow slightly guilty even when innocent?

*

I didn't hear about the attacks in Christchurch right away. That morning, the first time I check my mobile is on the way to drop off my son at nursery. He has decided to do a few more laps of the park on his bike, and as I wait for him I see a message from a friend telling me how shocked she is by the attacks, and asking how I feel about it.

I don't know how I feel. I only know that I can't and mustn't think about it, because I have to function for another few minutes and mime a happy world. I close the message and try to be here, in the moment, with my son, and not to let fear into our everyday life. I can only focus on what's happened once we have kissed each other goodbye on the cheeks and the forehead, like we do every morning.

I read the news. The attacker's video is everywhere. Scenes start playing automatically, scenes of people standing in the midst of the bloodbath screaming, crying or paralysed by fear. My eyes well up, but I'm sitting on a train and don't want to cry in front of strangers. I don't want their pity. I don't want to talk about it. I don't want to explain why I'm upset. So many others have already stood there, naked, showing their wounds, and been ridiculed for it. There's no need for new stories; everyone already knows all about it. The hatred is there for all to see, they just have to look at it.

We don't have to see people suffer to see them as people.

In May 2019, when Alabama passed a bill to outlaw abortion in almost all cases, the actor and producer Busy Philipps asked women to talk about their abortions on Twitter, using the hashtag #youknowme.[25] Thousands shared their experiences, but there were also voices arguing that they didn't have to reveal their experiences, that they shouldn't have to tell their story so that others would acknowledge them as human beings. One of them, the feminist Sara Locke, wrote, 'Here's the thing: #YouKnowMe, but I don't owe you my story. I don't owe you my private pain [...] for you to see me as a person. You owe me respect and autonomy over my body.'[26]

I did show my pain once. It was 2016, and I was about to give a talk on online hate speech, demanding 'organised love'.[27] That day, I no longer could, or wanted to, pretend that it didn't hurt. I kept crying even while I wrote my speech. So I rehearsed it in my hotel room. It should be passionate, yes, but I didn't want to express any emotion directly – there would be no tears rolling down my cheeks. I read the speech five times. The sixth time, my eyes remained dry.

I struggled on stage. I paused. Started again. The tears came. I paused again. Eventually, I couldn't hold back my tears – so I raced through the speech as quickly as possible. I was embarrassed. I couldn't accept the audience's applause afterwards. I didn't want to accept it.

I decided never to show my tears in public again.

Two years later, I was speaking in an idyllic little church in Switzerland. The pastor, a dedicated, sensitive man, asked me to stay on after my talk. Speaking in such a beautiful place, in front of people who had opened their minds and hearts to me, had been enough to move me, and when a band and choir started performing – reciting the words of the theologian and anti-fascist resistance fighter Dietrich Bonhoeffer – I closed my eyes. Suddenly, I realised that the choir had picked up words from my speech. I didn't dare open my eyes now. I struggled and struggled with myself. So far, so good; not a tear rolled down my cheek.

I'd succeeded.

Only after many conversations with friends and loved ones did I wake up from this 'success'. Islamic philosophy says that tears cleanse and soften the heart. No matter how much it hurts to expose yourself, sometimes a single tear says more than a thousand words. Especially in times of deafening silence.

As Martin Luther King, Jr. once said, 'History will have to record that the greatest tragedy [...] was not the strident clamor of the bad people, but the appalling silence of the good people.'[28] As long as the silence is followed by tears, I will dare to hope.

7

The Right-Wing Agenda

Words can be like tiny doses of arsenic;
and after a while, there's an effect.

Victor Klemperer, LTI: A Philologer's Notebook[1]

The right wing increasingly determines what we talk about. It dictates the topics we concern ourselves with, and the manner in which we interact with each other. It pursues domination through the tyranny of constant repetition, until we end up believing in the importance of the things it wants us to care about. Until we forget who we are.

This is happening under the radar. The rules that used to govern political discourse no longer apply in the new digital age, and we are forfeiting our ambiguities and contradictions. The contexts in which we live out the various facets of our personality – at work, among friends and family or in our spare time – have merged into a single space, and the different aspects of our personalities have frozen into a single identity. What we write, share and do in public is there for everyone – our relatives, colleagues, friends, acquaintances and strangers – to see. Yet how can the childishness and maturity, fragility and confidence, solidity and weakness, rationality and irrationality inside us possibly coexist in a public digital sphere where there can be no forgetting, where everything can always be unearthed, as if our past were also our present? How can we keep creating our selves, if we're caught up in an identity reflected back at us by the internet's mirror?

This new, unfree world is creating a polarised discourse which leaves hardly any room for us to take up positions that cannot be assigned to this or that camp. The internet exposes the ugly face of society. It makes visible the hatred that was once visible only to those directly affected by it. 'Fucking foreigners!' 'Slut!' The encounter is brief; someone mumbles the words in your ear, and there are no witnesses. Online, however, this fleeting moment in which the hater reveals their hatred to the hated finds an echo chamber, is repeated and radicalised – and thus becomes *permanently* public. Hate becomes the new normal.

Haters believe that they have the right to hate – and we let them provoke us. We confront those who are becoming ever more extremist, and thereby designate them our interlocutor. The prevailing mood is one of irritation: according to the media scholar Bernhard Pörksen, we take other people's reactions and behaviour as our constant point of reference, 'because we consider the other side's outrage to be the true irritant'; this results in the '*sensationalisation of outrage*, escalating in waves'.[2] Scandalised and exhausted, we seek the support of those who agree with us. Society becomes increasingly fragmented, and we drift further and further apart.

Even as we demand more empathy, tougher laws, culture change, civil courage, better police training and much more, we have to admit that we're feeling our way in the dark: the digital architecture that shapes these developments is opaque; we assume and speculate, but the algorithms of the most widely used social media platforms are hidden from the public eye. Imagine an eccentric dinner party, at which neither you nor any of the other guests understand the rules governing the conversation, despite the fact that you are all taking part in it. You have no idea why the insightful comments coming from the woman sitting next to you are so muffled that almost no one else at the table can hear them. You have no idea why another guest's amusing family video is being passed around the table for hours on end. You have no idea why one contribution suddenly drowns out all others. You have no idea why someone you barely know, who only a moment ago was sitting at the other end of the table, is suddenly by your side, insisting on showing you old wedding and holiday snaps. For some reason, the language around the table is getting coarser. Someone flies into a rage, and the mood switches. One man is holding up a tweet from a female politician and yelling across the table, another man is waving a blog entry from last week. The others, outraged, yell back. It's chaos.

What we ought to be asking ourselves is: why are we happy to play a game whose rules we don't understand? There are plenty of reasons not to.

When the UK voted to leave the EU in 2016, the journalist Carole Cadwalladr travelled to the small Welsh town of Ebbw Vale to find out more.[3] She wanted to know why over 60 per cent of eligible voters in this traditionally left-wing former steel town, with one of the lowest levels of immigration in the country, chose Brexit. She described how one woman 'told me about all this stuff that she'd seen on Facebook [...] she said it was all this quite scary stuff about immigration, and especially about Turkey', which was supposedly on the brink of joining the EU. In fact, though, the negotiations had been suspended for years. Cadwalladr scoured Facebook but found nothing – until she heard about the so-called dark ads, that is, Facebook posts which are never archived and can only be seen by the people who produce them and the people at whom they're targeted. Which means that journalists and researchers can't view the content being used to woo – or rather, manipulate – users.

Using conventional methods, it's impossible to pinpoint which social developments the medium of the internet has triggered or accelerated. Powerless and puzzled, we look on as a perfect breeding ground for one-dimensional world views develops. It's a paradise for fanatics and extremists of every shade.

Do we wholly comprehend the threat these developments pose? What happens if we waste all our energy fighting against an increasingly extremist political opponent, if we absorb only whatever confirms our world view, and if Google and Facebook, the gatekeepers of our age, use their algorithms to continually show us the things they think we want to see?[4]

How can we still agree on shared norms and coexist peacefully in society when people who supposedly speak the same language increasingly fail to get through to each other, because their value systems aren't compatible? How can we prevent the right from exploiting our outrage for its own purpose?

Outrage is a fundamentally important and useful social impulse. Picture this: a man enters a restaurant and starts shouting at the staff. The other diners give him disparaging looks and vigorously shake their heads. Some intervene. The momentary attention they pay to the man shouting at the staff has a corrective function: they are signalling to him that they won't tolerate behaviour like that. He will probably either leave the restaurant – still fuming – or be thrown out, or change his behaviour and apologise. Yet if the same man were to vent his anger on social media, he would not be sanctioned. Quite the opposite: his outrage would increase his reach. The more vigorous the reaction to his behaviour, the more eyes are on him and the more people listen to him; we mistake having a large audience for importance and relevance. With each provocative post, each wave of outrage, his platform grows. And then we wonder how he ended up being so famous and influential.

This process is characterised not only by a proliferation of messages without any news value, but also by the phenomenon of hotheads in positions of political power. Deliberate and aggressive provocation has the potential to lever the unscrupulous into the highest political office; and while thoughtfulness, mindfulness and restraint are punished with indifference, our attention is captured by ever more extreme positions. We thus have to deal with radicalised young people who think there is a 'holy war' going on and want to join IS in Syria; others who believe that there is a 'creeping Islamisation' afoot and civil war is inevitable, and feel called upon to set fire to refugee shelters; heterosexual men who call themselves incels, 'involuntary celibates', who think that they have the right to have sex and blame women for the fact that they don't, and take up arms; and others yet who believe in all seriousness that they only need light to survive, and die because of it.

However, when we talk about hatred in society, when we talk about conspiracy theorists or extremists, we often do it with the arrogance and condescension of people who believe that they, the social mainstream, are still fine. In truth, our perception has changed dramatically too.

How often have I heard it said in recent years that topics such as Islam, racism, women's rights, feminism, immigration and refugees 'are inherently polarising topics'? Not so. They are not polarising in themselves – they only become so when inflammatory posts on blogs and forums and in overflowing comment sections start shaping public discourse. Having said that, the plethora of hate-filled comments by no means reflects the plurality of opinion circulating in society; rather, they are deliberately and systematically marshalled by racist groups and right-wing populists. The Institute for Strategic Dialogue analysed more than 3,000 German media articles and more than 14,000 German-language comments on Facebook, and discovered that just 5 per cent of accounts are responsible for 50 per cent of all hate speech.[5] Research also suggests that certain niche platforms, such as 4chan and Gab, are prone to significantly higher percentages of abusive and aggressive content.[6] Discussions usually start off in these spaces, creating a community and gaining momentum, before moving on to other platforms. These are the people who write to specific publications and comment on selected articles in order to create the impression that certain views on Islam, immigration, women and refugees are socially untenable, too marginal and provocative for the social mainstream.[7] As a result, there is a shift in what we perceive to be 'normal' and defensible – even those who think that they're merely watching the punch-up from the sidelines are being changed by it.

Imagine you're sitting in the audience listening to a lecturer with whom you happen to agree. Yet a few seats along, two rows in front of you, over there in the right-hand corner of the room and directly behind you, there are people who keep heckling and shaking their heads in disbelief, evidently outraged by what's being said. What you don't know is that it's all part of a plan, to make it look as if a substantial part of the audience disagrees with the speaker. By the end of the evening, you almost inevitably think that what the speaker said must be – at the very least – controversial. This is how the desire for a fairer society becomes *controversial*. This is how altruism becomes *controversial*. And this is how we suddenly end up living in a society in which it is those who save others from drowning in the Mediterranean who have to justify their actions, rather than those who refuse to help.

That is what the commentators are aiming at in those forums. Their goal is not to respond to the authors, but to influence their fellow readers. They are targeting us, the readership. By constantly reiterating racist, xenophobic, anti-Semitic, anti-Muslim and anti-democratic positions they make them acceptable. They style themselves as heroes who boldly express supposed taboos and rebel against a 'politically correct' society where 'opinions' are being 'suppressed'.

And we legitimise them by reacting so expansively to their provocation. We credit their positions with relevance, and elevate racism, sexism, anti-Semitism and homophobia to legitimate ways of looking at the world – to 'opinions'. Day in, day out, we let them tell us what we should care about. Our days fill up; right-wingers and racists determine our social agenda and assign us homework – which we obediently complete.

*

Imagine if we took up the language of Islamist extremists: non-Muslim people would henceforth be known as unbelievers, *kuffar*; the 9/11 attackers would be 'heroes'; British or US troops would be called *salibiyoun*, 'armies of the crusaders'; our leaders would be *taghouts*, illegitimate rulers; and we'd call extremists *mujahidun*: people engaged in the Lord's struggle. Can you imagine that? Or doesn't it matter whose point of view our language adopts?

Indeed, some speech is adopted easily by the broader culture, and its original point of view erased: 'woke' was a word originally used by Black Americans to warn each other to stay vigilant in the face of white supremacy. Appropriated first by allies, then by the wider culture, it has become a byword for a world view centred on social

justice, equity and liberation; and now it has been wea-
ponised by the right, to demonise those who care about
these issues. The moment that a term like 'woke' is transformed into an insult we start looking at dedicated and
tolerant people through right-wing eyes, putting them in a
cage, homogenising a broad and heterogeneous spectrum
of people and reducing them to just a facet or two. When
people started using the term this way, people who had
never before been labelled found out what it is like to be
caged, to be reduced to a category. This is also why terms
like 'old white man' or 'gammon' cause such fury among
those labelled by them. Their reaction acts like a mirror,
showing them how debasing and discouraging it is when
other people think of you merely as a category.

In itself, the fact that right-wing populists describe
people who are committed to helping refugees, or eco-
activists, as 'woke lefties' isn't a problem. It becomes one
only when this particular use of the word crosses over
from right-wing language into general political discourse,
and when those who are disparagingly called 'woke' are
discouraged by it. Who wants to be 'naive' or 'reckless',
who wants to be taken advantage of because they're
'soft-hearted'? Who doesn't want to be 'rational', 'realis-
tic', 'practical' and 'tough'? Many have ended up asking
themselves: am I too left-wing? Too Green? Too tolerant? Too helpful? Too nice? Too trusting? Too naive? And
many compensate for such accusations with an exagger-
ated toughness and coldness. In that moment, plurality,
commitment and tolerance cease to be seen as desirable
qualities and are replaced by the urge to conform, and the

wish to please those whose goodwill you can only gain by sacrificing yourself. When someone dares to speak of values and morals they roll their eyes, exasperated. Only 'woke' people talk about those things.

> #Commie, #elitest, #leftisthack, #zealot, #betamale, #cuck, #culturalmarxist, #buildthatwall, #KAG #snowflakes #rapefugees #whitegenocide #socialjus-ticewarrior #DarkEnlightenment #libtard #beta #TheGreatReplacement #gayagenda

Each of these terms forces us to see the world from the point of view of right-wing ideology. As early as 1935, Bertolt Brecht understood that our choice of words either supports or resists fascism: 'Anyone in our times who says *population instead of "Volk" and land ownership instead of "soil"* is already denying his support to many lies. He divests the words of their lazy mysticism.'[8] Merely the con-scious refusal to use right-wing terms can therefore already be an act of resistance, a refusal to consider the world in terms of their ideology, which is dyed in hatred, dehuman-ising and desensitising.

In her 2009 book *Deutschland Schwarz Weiß* ('Germany Black [and] White'), the writer and activist Noah Sow explains how 'imprecise language helps to maintain the racist status quo':

> You do this, for example, when you don't use the term 'racism' because the word makes you flinch. When you do that, it's a sign that you would rather block out

racism and prefer not to name it. It's what happens, for instance, whenever the words 'anti-foreign', 'xeno-phobic' and 'right-wing extremist' are wrongly used in connection with racially motivated crimes. Yet ignoring or not wanting to think about racism is a sub-stantial obstacle to overcoming it.[9]

That this remains valid today becomes evident when-ever people talk about 'xenophobia' rather than racism.[10] Our choice of words must not be determined by an urge to preserve language; we must think carefully about the ideologies and injustices they prop up. In this sense, a just language is precisely *not* concerned with special interests – but with the right of language to change, to let itself be guided by human rights, justice and equality.

There are people who act as if it were rather daring of them to use 'politically incorrect' language. People like that are neither being conservative nor upholding tradition – they aren't really fighting against political correctness, but against justice. By insisting on using exclusionary language, they aren't being rebellious but *obeying the decree of oppression*. They are professing their desire to exclude people.

The author and activist Tupoka Ogette argues that in Western democratic countries 'there is no language police or censorship'. Everyone is allowed to say what they like – but we also have to take responsibility for what we do say: 'When you use the N-word, do it in the full knowledge that you're being deliberately racist and hurting people with it. You are no longer innocent.'[11]

By insisting on using exclusionary language in the face

of the current push for a more just one, you admit that you want to exclude people and are consciously taking up a position that is *against* fairness, *against* equality – and *for* a racist, sexist and xenophobic use of language.

Sometimes those on the right let slip terms that they never intended us to hear, and which reveal their true feelings – such as when the leader of the AfD described his party as an 'action group'.[12] At other times, they deliberately twist semantics, the meaning of words, to fit their world view.[13] In March 2021, the US conservative activist and writer Christopher F. Rufo tweeted: 'We have successfully frozen their brand – "critical race theory" – into the public conversation and are steadily driving up negative perceptions. We will eventually turn it toxic, as we put all of the various cultural insanities under that brand category.'[14] In a follow-up tweet, Rufo continues: 'The goal is to have the public read something crazy in the newspaper and immediately think "critical race theory". We have decodified the term and will recodify it to annex the entire range of cultural constructions that are unpopular with Americans.'[15] And so he and dozens of right-wing writers and thinkers did exactly that: they redefined critical race theory as something it is not, vilified and demonised it – creating a new bogeyman. In June 2021, the former president Donald Trump wrote an op-ed in which he claimed that students across the US 'are being subjected to a new curriculum designed to brainwash them with the ridiculous left-wing dogma known as "critical race theory"';[16] Senator Ted Cruz argued that 'critical race theory says every white person is a racist';[17] and Alabama state legislator Chris

Pringle asserted that 'it basically teaches that certain children are inherently bad people because of the color of their skin'.[18] None of this is true, but dozens of academics, journalists and writers spent weeks and months proving that it isn't. As the writer Ibram X. Kendi points out, 'the American people aren't divided. The American people are *being* divided. Republican operatives [...] have conjured an imagined monster to scare the American people and project themselves as the nation's defenders from that fictional monster'.[19] This perverted debate probably hit rock-bottom when some neo-conservative writers and politicians in all seriousness blamed critical race theory for the Taliban's victory in Afghanistan in the summer of 2021[20] – instead of the US's foreign politics and twenty years of war in Afghanistan.[21] Cynical.

Ever since an openly racist and sexist man became US president, an openly racist party with openly right-wing extremist members entered the German parliament and an openly racist party entered UK mainstream politics, the media's response to these parties' and individuals' provocations and discriminatory, divisive demagoguery has attracted increasingly vocal criticism. And we'll have to face the fact that we've allowed ourselves to be conned by deliberately provocative statements. In 2008, we extensively discussed whether Barack Obama was actually born in the US – taking resources and attention away from topics that were actually important and relevant to the presidential race. In 2016, when UKIP leader Nigel Farage posed in front of a poster depicting hundreds of migrants with the words 'Breaking Point', he incited fear and forced the debate on imaginary masses of migrants moving to the UK into the political arena – taking resources and attention away from topics that were actually important and relevant to the subject of Brexit.[22] When AfD leader Alexander Gauland declared in 2016 that 'people' wouldn't want the German footballer Jérôme Boateng as their neighbour, German media spent much time discussing whether Boateng would be a good neighbour to have. Some contributors argued that they would very much like him to live next door, others made fun of Gauland, others still did online interviews with Boateng's former neighbours, or conducted supposedly light-hearted surveys in which they asked passers-by whom they would prefer as a neighbour, Boateng or Gauland. So the question whether Black people make good neighbours actually became a bona fide topic of discussion. It was disgraceful.

Why is it that such provocations succeed? Let's ask ourselves: why do we feel called upon to react? Because such provocations are our chance to feel morally superior? Because we believe that it's a journalist's duty? Because we don't realise that our outrage is their currency? Because we assume that they possess an ounce of decency? Because things are 'finally getting exciting', and we're secretly, voyeuristically, exhilarated by all that ignominy?

It is because of us that right-wing nationalists and populists have come to power in our countries. We have legitimised their provocations by discussing them, we have granted their hatred the status of an opinion and we have elevated their xenophobia, racism, anti-Semitism and sexism to the ranks of legitimate points of view.

*

What is interesting, and disappointing, is that I recognise the process from the many Muslim communities in the West who, especially after 9/11, invested a large part of their energy in responding to attacks from outside: attacks from Islamist extremists who claimed to be acting in the name of all Muslims, and from the public media and politicians who criminalised and stigmatised Muslims and reduced them to the actions of those extremists – thus confirming the extremists' claim that they are the only true representatives of Islam.

We expended much of our time, energy, effort and attention on explaining the obvious. We answered the most absurd questions and distanced ourselves from the atrocities, although the mere suggestion that we supported the killing, bloodshed, suffering, brutality and horror in any way whatsoever is demeaning.

'Don't take it personally,' they said when we pointed out how hurtful such accusations are. 'Don't get so emotional.' So we suppressed our feelings, so as not to deepen the irrational fears of worried citizens.

Now, as I look back nearly two decades later, I can see that our constant defensiveness meant that we neglected internal discussions about Islam. Fearing that someone might instrumentalise such discussions, we insufficiently criticised any misconduct – sexism, anti-Semitism, extremism, racism – within our communities. Afraid to add fuel to the fire, we didn't even throw water on it.

Over the years, we therefore risked losing sight of

ourselves, of what moved *us* – from within ourselves. We spoke less and less *to* each other, and more and more *about* each other, in public. We ran out of space for conversations in which we didn't have to compete to make ourselves heard and be certified as a *good* Muslim by a non-Muslim audience.

I wonder: what if we cared less about what others think of us and our religion? What would we focus on then? Would we deal differently with those who are weaponising our religion – who are exploiting our coexistence, our plurality and not least our children as ammunition for their wars and violent fantasies? Would we focus on education rather than rhetoric, and on knowledge instead of defensive battles? For it is our constant defensive pose that makes us homogeneous.

The same pattern is now being repeated within the majority society: by allowing right-wing populists and extremists to dictate the political agenda, we have neglected the things that are actually important. They set the topic and we react, obediently and predictably.

And so the young people who are taking to the streets in increasing numbers are, among other things, also protesting against the right's monopoly on our attention, and the government politicians who are giving in to it. Climate, the environment, education, health, social and generational justice, protecting minority rights – then, as now, these issues are being neglected in favour of the topics that the right wants us to talk about. And when they are talked about, the discussion merely expends itself on the question of whether these issues and injustices exist in the first place.

There's a reason why right-wingers deny climate change. There's a reason why they are keen to prevent us from looking at the world in a way that will lead to solidarity with the poorest countries and people around the world. If we take climate change seriously, national interest will inevitably be superseded by the awareness that, while there are many different countries, states and nations in the world, we are *one* common human race living on *one* common planet.

What to do? How do we face up to right-wingers without involuntarily empowering them through our response? For example, by confronting them with the consequences of their words, by unmasking their strategies, by not falling for their claim that they are 'the voice of the people', by not adopting their terms, and by not pursuing their logic. By making it clear that our political language is the battlefield of an extremist right-wing 'action group', where we fight about through whose eyes we look at society, whom we consider to be one of us, our friend – and whom we consider to be an alien, an enemy. As Victor Klemperer wrote, we don't speak the 'language of the victor [...] with impunity; we inhale and live up to it'.[23]

We have to stop responding, and instead prioritise those issues and questions that can move society forward. If we merely react, we hand the political playing field over to people of action while we degenerate into perpetual prey. In a 2004 article, the investigative journalist Ron Suskind quotes one of George W. Bush's political advisers as saying:

We're an empire now, and when we act, we create our

own reality. And while you're studying that reality [...]
we'll act again, creating other new realities, which you
can study too [...]. We're history's actors [...] and you,
all of you, will be left to just study what we do.[24]

It doesn't take a global power to control culture and discourse, to dictate what the public ought to care about.
Even as right-wing extremists cast themselves in the part
of the underdog, as the brave, marginalised, excluded,
poor, piteous representatives of the 'little people' and the
'real people of this country', they are creating new realities – and we go along with it. We react. React. React. Until
we've forgotten who we are.

8

The Illusion of Sovereignty

> Man [...] is not present in any subject: for manhood
> is not present in the individual man.
>
> *Aristotle,* Categories[1]

The world has no need for categories – it is we who need them. We construct categories to navigate this complex, contradictory world of ours, to somehow understand it and communicate it to each other.

We need categories. If anyone tried to perceive everything in this world unfiltered and uncategorised – people both known and unknown, animals large and small, smells and noises, all that information with which we're inundated – they would simply be flooded by stimuli, and drown in them.

We need categories. Cataloguing and categorising our environment helps us to recognise patterns, to make quick decisions and react to situations, especially dangerous ones. In moments like that, we draw on images and information we stored up long before. Seeing the world in terms of categories is therefore a necessity.

Yet at what point do the categories that we construct in order to make the world comprehensible turn into cages? When does our freedom become someone else's captivity?

Imagine the spectrum of colours – of all those beautiful colours, moving from red to orange to yellow to green to blue to indigo to violet, and again: red, orange, yellow … We all know very well that we could have endless discussions about whether a particular colour is already orange or still red, whether it's green or blue, and we know that there are many more colours in between. And so we know that these categories, the names for the colours that we have created in our languages, are incapable of covering the beauty of nature in all of its facets. These names, these categories, are nothing but incomplete, flawed, limited attempts by us humans to capture a fraction of the beauty of this world. Now imagine these colours, their names and categories, as absolute categories inhabiting the illusion of sovereignty.

It is the illusion of sovereignty that makes cages of categories, i.e. the presumptuous notion that our own narrow, limited world view is complete, entire and universal, and the arrogant belief that we can wholly comprehend another person in all their complexity, that we can even wholly understand an entire constructed *category* of people. More than 70 million people become *the* refugee, 1.9 billion people become *the* Muslim and half the world's population becomes *the* woman. *The* Black man. *The* woman with a disability. *The* homosexual. *The* migrant worker. *The* non-binary person.

No one, no single person or society can claim to know everything. And yet it is what certain people, ideologies and cultures claim – at times violently and blatantly, sometimes more softly and subtly – leading to the assumption of authority and thence to oppression. As Michel Foucault said, 'Where there is power, there is resistance.'[2]

Where does this illusion of sovereignty come from? Ordinarily, people don't consciously decide to despise specific people or groups of people, and to rob them of their humanity. Rather, we are raised to think that way – all of us, regardless of whether we suffer or benefit from these mechanisms. We are raised to think that the walls that enclose us are immovable, which is why we don't realise that our perspective is limited; rather, we regard it as all-encompassing.

Our thoughts and perceptions are shaped so subtly that we rarely notice it happening. The cognitive psychologist John Bargh has examined the ways in which we are unconsciously influenced in our behaviour, and provided powerful examples showing that independent, autonomous action is to some degree an illusion. For example, our first impression of someone is affected by our prior experience of physical warmth or coldness: Bargh describes an experiment in which the participants were greeted by an associate of his team and taken to the lab. On the way there, the associate would ask each participant to briefly hold a cup of either hot or iced coffee while she filled in a form. The participants held the cup for about ten seconds. When they arrived at the lab, they were asked to read a description of a person, and to rate that person's personality traits. The results showed that those who had held a cup of hot coffee rated the so-called target person as 'warmer' than those who had held a cup of iced coffee.[3]

Another example is the manner in which architecture

and town planning determine how we behave in public spaces. We traverse the topography of the urban landscape as if mechanically, adhering to the traffic rules we internalised at a young age: pedestrians belong on the pavement, bicycles on the cycle path, cars on the road. If you stray, you are sanctioned. How we get from A to B is so tightly regulated that with time we even learn to ignore our natural instincts.

You find out how true this is when you are out and about with a small child. The child doesn't consciously run 'into the street' – it simply hasn't yet grasped that there is a difference between streets, pavements and cycle paths. The child also thinks it odd that when the light changes it's supposed to cross the very same street that it wasn't allowed to step into a moment ago, even though the dangerous cars about which it's constantly being warned are still approaching left and right. When my son was about two years old, whenever we crossed a busy road he would put up a hand to the approaching cars and signal for them to stop. He still had to learn that the shining lights we call 'traffic lights' are there to convey the notion of safety – absurd though it might be – and to let a green light override his instinct for danger.

Traffic rules make sense, of course, but that's not the point – the point is that we need to be more acutely aware of how the shape of our environment is designed to shape our perception. Let's take another example from town planning: so-called hostile or aggressive architecture, whose aim is to keep tourist sites free from visible poverty and social inequality. Have you noticed that some park benches are divided by arm rests? Many people consider them a welcome innovation – not knowing that their primary purpose is not to relieve your tired forearms, but to prevent homeless people from sleeping on them. That's how one type of social reality – visible signs of poverty and the gaps in our welfare system – disappears from the field of view of people who aren't affected by it. Urban design is being used to push the homeless out of public spaces, without those who do have a home ever noticing.

I myself only noticed it when someone pointed it out to me. Similarly, it took a long time for me to notice the extent to which our architecture impairs wheelchair users. A few years ago, I invited some friends over to celebrate my birthday, among them a few who use wheelchairs. Afterwards, I wondered whether they would actually be able to access our flat. I was worried. How thoughtless of me not to check beforehand. Having taken some measurements and asked around, I was relieved to discover that, yes, they would be able to get into the building, and also through the front door to our flat. However, they wouldn't be able to access the toilet. In the end, a hotel down the street offered to make its accessible toilets available to our guests.

It was an enlightening experience. Once again, I felt what it means to be privileged, and learnt that we can't overcome restrictive social structures with good intentions and individual effort alone. We need to ask ourselves for *whom* we are fashioning our world – not only our towns and cities, our infrastructure and building layout, but technology, politics, economy, security and medical care.

Did you know that only one in eight women suffers chest pains during a heart attack? The oft-described shooting pain is a far more common symptom in men, while women tend to feel nauseous or experience pains in the jaw, shoulders or back.[4] Furthermore, in the case of men, it takes on average twenty minutes for a heart attack to be diagnosed and medical treatment to be arranged; in the case of women it takes forty to forty-five minutes, i.e. twice as long. Women are therefore at a greater risk of dying from a heart attack than men. The reason for the discrepancy is simply that more research has been done on heart attacks in men.[5] Caroline Criado Perez describes the absence of sufficient data relating to women, in this as in many other fields, as the 'gender data gap'. She argues that this lack of information is no accident, because most of the data we use to evaluate the different areas of our lives comes from male bodies.[6]

When I raised the variation in heart attack mortality rates during a panel discussion, two doctors approached me about it afterwards. They said it couldn't be true – that the symptoms of a heart attack were the same, regardless of gender. It was as if they felt personally attacked as professionals.

Yet we are *all* limited, and showing someone their limitedness doesn't constitute an attack. Everyone should be aware of their limits – *especially* people with an above-average education and considerable expertise. If someone has spent years acquiring specialist knowledge, they should also know that learning everything is an impossible task, and that opening our eyes to the architecture of our being is a good thing: it's an opportunity to see the walls that divide us from the rest of the world.

*

> It has become patently clear that the stability of states and
> religions simply does not primarily rest on institutions,
> not even on power and violence, but on something entirely
> different: the humility of the humiliated. This resource
> is now coming to an end. It has been almost completely
> exhausted, and that's why the earth is quaking.
>
> *Bernd Ulrich,* Good Morning, Occident[7]

Aren't the labellers maybe just *curious* about the people behind those glass walls? Aren't they simply interested in where they come from (that is, *really* come from), in how they love and live, what they believe and feel? No, they aren't: because so long as their belief in the sovereignty of their perception remains untouched, that kind of curiosity is nothing but an aspect of the scrutiny to which the labelled are subjected, a way to exert power.

If their curiosity were free from power, both labellers and labelled would be asking each other questions – respectfully, and on an equal footing. Both would be sitting at the table; neither would be lying on it, analysed and scrutinised. It wouldn't be a case of one of them stripping while the other looks on with interest, or even goes so far as to tear the clothes off the person who is being appraised, scrutinises them and – may I? – check their 'muzzle'.

One night, as I was on a train travelling from Berlin to

Hamburg, a young white man sat down next to me. He was involved in the Fridays for Future climate movement. He said he was a fan of my work, and asked if I would provide a statement for their upcoming conference. We got talking. After a while an elderly white man joined in, and asked the young man whether he belonged to any political party. The young man replied hesitantly and then asked the elderly man the same question, but the latter was evasive and instead mentioned the name of a left-wing magazine, where he apparently worked. Then the elderly man turned to me and asked, 'What about you?' I said that I wasn't a member of any party. He replied, 'Nah, I meant where've you come from?' 'How do you mean – from which event?' I asked, because we'd just been talking about an event that the young man had attended. He shook his head and gave me a meaningful smile. 'Do you want to know which town I'm from?' I asked. Silence. He continued smiling, undeterred. 'You want to know what country my parents are from?' I asked. The young man, embarrassed, had sunk into his seat. The elderly man nodded. I sighed. 'My parents are originally from Turkey,' I said. And as if on cue, he shot back: 'And you? You're traditional and religious, yes?'

Irritated, I turned away. The young man cringed a little further into his seat; but all of a sudden he sat up and asked me, loudly, so that everyone around us could hear, 'So, what event have you just come from?'

Why does his question suggest a respectful curiosity, while that of the elderly man can only be described as scrutiny? Because the young man was asking no more of me than what he himself was prepared to divulge. Because he hadn't asked me in order to categorise me, but because he was interested in me as a person. From the start, he had approached me as an individual. Had it been somehow relevant to our conversation – had we been talking about multilingualism, for instance – he could naturally have asked me about my parents and grandparents too. The elderly man, however, was only interested in confirming his preconceptions about 'women like me'.

Some kinds of curiosity are more equal than others. Some categorisations are more equal than others. It is the illusion of sovereignty that makes the difference. It is the illusion of sovereignty that dehumanises the object of curiosity.

Thomas Bauer, a scholar of Islam and Arabic studies, calls this conviction an 'urge to universalise', which is antithetical to an awareness of perspective; he takes his inspiration from Friedrich Nietzsche's assertion that we can only look at things subjectively, never objectively – and that 'objectivity' can only be approached through a 'diversity of perspectives'.[8] To impose our own point of view on others, Nietzsche argues, is a 'ludicrous presumption'.[9]

How can we put these ideas into practice? How can we enrich existing knowledge with other points of view? How can we enable thought processes and cognitive processes that include a variety of views right from the start? Bauer here proposes the concept of 'cultural ambiguity':

The phenomenon of cultural ambiguity exists when, over an extended period of time, a practice or object is assigned two contradictory – or at any rate two competing and clearly divergent – meanings simultaneously; when a social group draws the norms and meanings that govern specific aspects of life simultaneously from opposing, or widely divergent, discourses; or when a group simultaneously accepts different interpretations of a phenomenon, and no interpretation can claim exclusive validity.[10]

Bauer describes the Renaissance as one such example from European history, when an admiration for pagan antiquity was rarely seen as contradicting Christianity. Arabic society shows up a remarkably large number of instances of a cultural tolerance of ambiguity – for instance, Middle Eastern literature between the twelfth and nineteenth centuries considered successful experiments in ambiguity and a sparkling style as a sign of artistic talent and scholarship.

Bauer gives the example of the nineteenth-century Christian Lebanese scholar and poet Nasif al-Yaziji, whose literary ambiguity was criticised by the German Arabist Heinrich Leberecht Fleischer, a contemporary of Al-Yaziji's. Bauer calls Fleischer's criticism a 'prime example' not only 'of the modern West's condemnation of ambiguity, but also of the Western urge to universalise':[11]

Sheikh Nasif [al-Yaziji] was one of the key representatives of the literature of his time. He was a Greek Catholic, and very much open to Western ideas. Yet he steadfastly continued in the classical tradition in his writing and scholarship – much to the distress of Western authors such as Fleischer, who admired Al-Yaziji in principle, but thought his persistence in the tradition a grave error. He believed that its main problem was its very delight in ambiguity – or, as Fleischer described it, that 'fruitless playing at art' – which is characteristic of all Al-Yaziji's works.[12]

Yet the ambiguity that Bauer describes affects not only the meanings of words. What is particularly fascinating is the question of how we label people.

Whom do we describe as 'foreign'? The *OED* defines the term among other things as 'pertaining to, characteristic of, or derived from another country or nation; not domestic or native'. But how do we *know* that someone is 'from another country or nation'? In terms of popular perception, the certainty is derived principally from external characteristics, such as someone's speech, dress or physiognomy. People are described as 'foreign' because they look or sound like this or that, and the naming, the categorisation, is thus executed without the labelled having had their say.

Can we imagine a different process of naming people?

Thomas Bauer describes a conversation said to have occurred in the year 1400 between the historian Ibn Khaldun and Amir Timur (Tamerlane). During an audience, Timur asked Ibn Khaldun what he could do for him. Ibn Khaldun replied:

'In this country, I am a foreigner in terms of two "foreign" places – the Maghrib, where I was born and raised, and Cairo, where my people are. I have now come into the realm of your shadow, and I ask you to tell me how I – in this, my foreignness – can attain familiarity.' 'Tell me what you desire,' countered Timur, 'and I will do it for you.' 'The condition of being foreign has made me forget what it is that I desire,' Ibn Khaldun replied. 'But perhaps you – may God give you strength – can tell me what I want.' [...]

Ibn Khaldun is not a foreigner because he is in Damascus, but because he is *not* in Tunis or in Cairo. That is why he doesn't talk about the *foreignness of Damascus* but of the *foreignness of Tunis and Cairo*.[13]

The remarkable thing here is that foreignness is not being defined by outsiders and simply ascribed to the one affected by it; the description is provided by the one affected himself.

This becomes even clearer in another of Bauer's examples. In 1325, the jurist and traveller Ibn Battuta arrived in Tunis, not far from his home town of Tangier. The cities shared a similar culture, and the same language was spoken in both. When he arrived, no one greeted him, and he was overwhelmed by a feeling of foreignness. In his account of his travels, he writes:

Now they all came forward to greet each other; I alone was not kissed by anyone, because no one knew me. I felt such a pain in my soul that I was unable to hold back my profuse tears, and cried bitterly. But one of the pilgrims saw how it was with me, and approached me with a greeting and comforted me with his company.[14]

Ibn Battuta's secretary added a further anecdote by another scholar, a traveller who had also arrived in a place where he wasn't greeted or welcomed. As in the case of Ibn Battuta, someone noticed this, hurried over to him and said, 'When I saw you standing apart from the others and that no one greeted you, I realised that you were a foreigner and wanted to comfort you with my company.' Bauer concludes:

> Here, too, the foreigner's foreignness is overcome by friendliness, or at least lessened by it. Classical Arab civilisation therefore did not perceive foreignness as a mark of origin, descent, race or language, but as an emotional need within the individual who feels foreign. It is thus not a permanent mark, either, but a condition that one can, in theory, overcome. Most importantly, foreignness is something apprehended by the person who considers themselves to be foreign. [...] Nowhere is the foreigner foreign because they have come from outside and are seen as not belonging 'here' because of their otherness.[15]

Could this provide a model for a way of speaking which incorporates the perspectives of those *with* whom and *about* whom we speak, so that they retain their own sovereignty? This means that no one would be subject to someone else's absolute power and sovereignty over definition.

You can certainly describe someone as a 'Black man' or a 'hijab-wearing woman'; tags like these are only problematic when they remain the sole identifier, even while there are other levels of perception to draw on.

Imagine a conference about feminism, where men constitute a minority. For the duration of the conference they are referred to homogeneously as 'men', and people keep getting them mixed up; they are continuously and solely acknowledged in terms of their gender.

Imagine an international business event attended by people from all over the world, where the team from your country constitutes a minority. For the duration of the event you are referred to homogeneously as 'the Brits', 'the Americans', or whatever your nationality might be, and people keep getting you mixed up; you are continuously and solely acknowledged in terms of your specific (supposed) origin, and stereotyped according to it.

Imagine if this experience wasn't temporary, if it didn't occur only now and again but constantly, throughout your entire life.

Can we conceive the Museum of Language differently – as a place where there is no one who isn't labelled, no one who represents an unquestioned norm, because *everyone* is both labeller and labelled; a place where everyone has the opportunity to speak in a way that makes others see the world through their eyes; a place where everyone can speak *freely*?

Then again, how can someone who has learnt to look at themselves through other people's eyes not only discover their own perspective, but put it into words?

How can we speak *freely*?

9

Speaking Freely

When one human being tells another human
being what is 'real', what they are actually
doing is making a demand for obedience.

Humberto Maturana[1]

A man once sent me a death threat. I was in my early twenties, and working as a columnist for a German daily. The comment section under my articles was a favourite haunt for hate-speech devotees, so I wasn't surprised when my first death threat landed in my inbox. Ah well, that was part of the deal. If you write, you will receive threats. The editors, alarmed, sent me to the police; the police sent me home with a shrug. Back then, the police knew even less than they do today what to make of the digital world.

I, meanwhile, found the threat rather interesting. It extended to two pages. On the first one and a half pages the author explained in detail why he, a 'Russo-German', was more German than I, a 'German Turk': his grandfather had worked and fought for Germany, and anyway, his family had been in the country a lot longer than mine. Then followed a lovingly detailed description of how he would put an end to my life. Fascinating.

Six months later, just after I got married, I wrote a column about love which didn't have any political or social message – at least, not intentionally. It was about a Turkish tradition according to which, when a man wants to propose, he and his family pay the prospective bride's family a visit. Her family serves everyone coffee with sugar – except him: he is handed a cup of coffee with salt in it. While the others happily sip their sweet coffee, they watch with amusement as the future groom swallows the salty coffee without wincing, as proof of his love.

When the column was published, I received lots of congratulatory messages. As well as a note from the author of the death threat. He began by saying that he may have scared me with his first email. Maybe just a tiny bit, I thought, and for the first time admitted to myself how crazy it was emotionally to normalise a death threat the way I had done. Then he apologised. He said that my column had made him realise that I, too, was merely human. Bravo, I thought. He might have thought of that sooner.

What had changed? Why was it that a man who just months earlier had sent me a message full of violent fantasies now saw the *human* in me? It was the love story that did it: it was a story without good or evil, without accusations or justifications, a *human* story. One in which I wasn't allowing myself to be scrutinised, in which I didn't explain myself – which I had written exactly as I would have told it to a friend. A piece in which I didn't court the sympathy of the unlabelled, but was simply a young woman writing about love.

The story had created a new space by giving the object

of hate a human face. The hater thus recognised himself in the face of the hated. He saw something of himself that he hadn't expected to find there; he saw himself through my eyes, and recognised himself as a hater. What enables us to hate *others* is their dehumanisation, which is enabled by crass language and biased images, and by the utter abstraction of other people's plight through scenarios, numbers and theses in which the plight of the individual disappears, becomes invisible – and the image we have of each other consequently grows blurry. We exist together in this world, but at the same time we are in a kind of trance. We are capable of abstracting people to such an extent that we no longer recognise them as human. Sometimes even when we are face to face with them. We look, but we no longer see.

Schools are usually the places where young people experience plurality as a reality rather than an abstract scenario. They aren't free of racism, but they put obstacles in the way of abstraction; these obstacles are called 'individual people'.

A friend once told me about her time at school during the 1980s. The son of a well-known local Nazi was in her class. One day, he and his clique stood at the school gates and separated the pupils into 'foreigners' (left) and 'Germans' (right). When my friend, a delicate Black girl, stood in front of him, he sent her to the right, with 'the Germans'.

'Why didn't you send me left, with the foreigners?' she asked him. 'Oh,' he said with a dismissive wave, 'I know you.'

He can't abstract her, because he sees her every day – he can no longer *not* see her.

Sometimes it works. A personal encounter can counteract abstract, vague fears. This phenomenon is called 'contact hypothesis', and it is said that frequent encounters with *others* – a group that is somehow *different*, whether in an ethnic, religious, social or any other sense – can break down prejudice.[2] I have often seen it work, the way that personal contact can make someone see another person. But I have also known the hypothesis to fail, and know what it's like to speak and not be heard, to stand in front of someone and look into their eyes, and for them *simply not to see you*.

I will never forget one particular experience. I was at a conference, when I ran into someone who had repeatedly and publicly made hateful comments about me. I approached her, because somewhere inside me there was a grain of hope that a face-to-face conversation might at least make the forthcoming debate less heated. It wasn't my first such encounter, yet in the past, whenever I looked into someone else's eyes and they into mine, we were able to see the *human being* behind the abstraction. True, we would continue to differ on fundamental matters, and there might be plenty of reasons why we couldn't stand each other; but we could respect each other as *people*, and remain detached and critical, but also fair – realising that we were both human, and as vulnerable as each other.

Yet this person didn't perceive me as a person. She kept talking in a hateful manner, full of disgust and disdain. She looked at me but didn't see me, listened but didn't hear me, and I felt a fear and helplessness I'd never known before. It took days for me to get over the encounter.

The man who had sent me the death threat had only been able to send it in the first place because he hadn't seen me as a person, but as the embodiment of his abstract fears. He had projected his fears on to me. My existence, my body, had made the intangible tangible. I had been a living symbol of what he loathed.

Yet all of a sudden he had apologised. Even today, I think about the moment the scales must have fallen from his eyes and he not only perceived me, the person, but also recognised his own face, the face of someone who hates.

This was the first lesson I learnt as a writer: *be* human. Write as a *human being*.

And yet it was years before I truly understood it. Years during which the debates and discourses that I engaged with tired me out and drained me of all vitality. Years during which I became part of the dehumanising system – instead of just being human.

In her speech entitled 'The Danger of the Single Story', the author Chimamanda Ngozi Adichie describes what happens when an entire continent is reduced to a single narrative; her story begins with Fide, a young man employed in her family's household. When she was a child, she had always thought of him as 'poor Fide'. One day, she visits him and his family in their village, and sees an entirely different side to him. He is now no longer 'poor Fide', but so much more: he is the child of a lively, musical family. Years later, as a student in the US, she again experiences 'poor' Fide's story, only now she is on the receiving end:

this time it is she, Chimamanda, the daughter of academics, whom her college room-mate pities, because she sees in her merely a girl from the 'poor' African continent. A few years later, when she was a fellow at a US university with several published books under her belt, one of her students told her 'that it was such a shame that Nigerian men were physical abusers', referring to a character in one of her novels. 'I told him that I had just read a novel called *American Psycho*, and that it was such a shame that young Americans were serial murderers.' Hardly anyone outside the US would generalise about its whole society based on novels like *American Psycho*, horror films or psychological thrillers. Perception of American society is multifaceted: thanks to US films, TV series, music and literature, millions around the world know what it is like to be born, live and die there. There is a rich, multi-dimensional perception of the culture and society – people don't know just *one* story about it, but *many*. 'The problem with stereotypes is not that they are untrue, but that they are incomplete. They make one story become the only story,' says Adichie.[3] If a single story dominates our perception of an entire group of people, they no longer exist as individuals. Defining people according to a given category isn't wrong so much as insufficient. *One* truth becomes the *only* truth.

The best way to illustrate the danger that a single story poses is to turn things on their head and make the labellers the labelled:

Old white men are sexist. Old white men who are directors, politicians, doctors, public officials, professors and teachers use their position of power to victimise others.

White men are paedophiles. They abduct children and lock them up in cellars, and white clerics abuse boys.

White carers are greedy. They asphyxiate old women with pillows to inherit their money.

White police officers are right-wing extremists.

White politicians lie about everything.

Rich white people are a burden on the state. They steal from the state by exploiting tax loopholes. They cheat to get their children into university.

White people are racist. They classify people into artificial categories of race, in order to judge them on the basis of their fiction. They colonise entire continents, enslave and abduct people, they steal their land and natural resources. And when their victims protest against racism, they accuse them of creating social division.

*

Ask yourself this: what truths about marginalised minorities are currently circulating? How multifaceted are the representations you see of Black sons, migrant fathers and Muslim grandmothers?

How can we apprehend someone as a human being, if they routinely enter our perception by means of a *single* story – a dehumanised, much distorted, stereotyped and negative narrative?

Some people grow into the narrow shell of the stereotype and threaten to suffocate in it, while others resist and wander like phantoms through a society that fears them. If you don't speak for yourself as a human being, you don't exist. Only your cliché lives.

I once met an intelligent middle-aged woman called Kader Abla, originally from Turkey, who told me about something that happened to her once and which I still think about today:

Kader Abla[4] lives in Germany, but doesn't speak German. She speaks many other languages, but not German. She is clever and well read, though not according to other people's definition. She is confident, which irritates those who consider her uneducated: it simply doesn't fit. When they see her, they see the hijab and wonder where her confidence comes from.

Her foster son, who has heart disease, is lying in hospital. The doctor enters the room, looks around, and begins to talk to the others in the room about her foster son – not to her, the foster mother. Kader wrestles with herself. She is seething. She reaches for sentences that slip through her fingers, and struggles with unfamiliar words that don't do justice to her feelings.

Silence.

Then, slowly, she leans forward, looks into the doctor's eyes and says:

'I am invisible.'

The doctor is embarrassed, exposed.

The moment she said 'I', she became visible.

She became herself.

*

Kader Abla's experience revealed to me once again how powerful speech is. By speaking, she turned from a mere outline into a person and forced her interlocutor to perceive her. As long as she remained silent, her body had no story. It was a displayed object.

In 'Stranger in the Village', James Baldwin describes how people reacted to him when he visited a small village in the Swiss Alps in 1951. He was the first Black man they'd ever seen. He smiled at them because, he writes, Black people in the US were taught to 'make people "like"' them. But smiling didn't work:

> No one, after all, can be liked whose human weight and complexity cannot be, or has not been, admitted. My smile was simply another unheard-of phenomenon which allowed them to see my teeth – they did not, really, see my smile and I began to think that, should I take to snarling, no one would notice any difference.[5]

Their inability to recognise him as a person rendered the inhabitants of the village unable to appreciate the universal language of the smile. Seventy years later, in 2020, the Black British barrister Alexandra Wilson arrived at court only to be stopped at the entrance by a security guard, who 'asked me what my name was so he could "find [my] name on the list" (the list of defendants)'.[6] She tried to shrug this off as an innocent mistake, but it was not the last time that Wilson's identity was mistaken that day: a member of the public tried to prevent her from entering the courtroom; inside, a lawyer tried to turn her away; and finally the clerk 'told me to leave the courtroom [...] [and] asked if I was represented'. For the fourth time that morning, Wilson had to explain that she was a defence barrister.

How are you supposed to react to this? How are you supposed to react, when it doesn't happen just once, but over and over again – because this kind of dehumanisation is systematic and called 'racism'? Wilson was eventually able to talk to the prosecutor and proceed with the case. But in the Twitter thread in which she recounts these events, she concludes: 'This really isn't OK though. I don't expect to have to constantly justify my existence at work.'

*

Why do I write? 'Cause I have to. 'Cause my voice,
in all its dialects, has been silent too long.

Jacob Sam-La Rose, Sable LitMag[7]

The artist and scholar Grada Kilomba says that, to her, Sam-La Rose's words illustrate 'writing as an act of *becoming*, and as I write, I *become* the narrator, and the writer of my own reality, the author of and the authority on my own history. In this sense, I become the absolute opposition of what the colonial project has predetermined.'[8]

Yet how can someone speak in such a way that they *really* speak, write in such a way that they *become*? How can they exist in a language that doesn't envisage them as a speaker, which isn't intended or fashioned for them? How can they speak without submitting themselves to scrutiny? How can they speak without describing themselves from someone else's point of view? These are questions I have been exploring throughout this book – and for my entire life.

On a cool and rainy afternoon, I was sitting in the office of the editor-in-chief of a major German paper. We were discussing a possible political column. 'What would I be allowed to write about?' I asked. 'Anything,' he replied. 'Anything?' I asked. 'Anything,' he repeated. I started testing the limits of this 'anything'. 'About economics too?' 'Yes.' 'And love?' 'Yes.' 'Arts and sports?' He interjected, 'Yes, Kübra. Anything.'

I sat there in his office, paralysed. I was overwhelmed. After a long pause, I told him, 'I feel like a bird that's lived in a cage for years and years. And now that the door is open, I realise I've forgotten how to fly.'

How do you *speak freely*, as a person, as an individual? I didn't know, and so I said nothing for a while.

My silence meant escaping from the prison of the individual languages in which I moved. I wanted to perceive myself outside them. I wanted to experience myself, get to the bottom of me, in the various languages and points of view that offered themselves up to me. I wanted to experience spirituality without justifying myself. I wanted to be *me*.

So I tried to find my way back to language. Through my own consciousness. I tried to find words for this experience and make room for new perceptions, not in order to explain them to others, but for myself, to pursue my need for expression. Not to be understood, but to exist.

Trying to find a new language can be overwhelming. New things can be scary, and the unknown can overburden us. But I also discovered that, if we create a space in which it can develop, a new language can suddenly become possible. For instance, on evenings such as the one on which three Muslim friends – an entrepreneur, a poet and a lawyer – came over to my place, and we had an intense discussion about our faith and spirituality. We talked with an intimacy that is rare when the topic is Islam, the hijab and suchlike. Our faith was the foundation on which we were able to express our differences too; we were connected by our experiences in the outside world, our age, the fact that we were women, our creative drive and our commitment to society. None of us was being scrutinised. It was a respectful conversation.

At the end of the evening, just as they were leaving, I proposed that we have this conversation in front of a virtual audience. So we went back into my living room, sat down, clicked on Instagram's 'Live' button and carried on talking. The audience grew minute by minute until, at one o'clock in the morning, more than 600 people were listening to us and joining in the discussion.

None of us was speaking as *the* Muslim woman, *the* hijab-wearer or *the* person from an immigrant background. The poet talked about how she expresses her faith and empowers herself and others through her poems, and the entrepreneur talked about changing careers. The audience asked questions, thought along with us and shared their experiences. What connected us was more than our being excluded – as Muslim women, people from an immigrant background and marginalised minorities: it was our experiences, and the interests, passions and dreams we were pursuing.

And there it was, the new language of which I had dreamt for years: the act of speaking to people who aren't pressurising me to make myself understood, but add their perspective to my stories and my thoughts. The act of speaking to people to whom I don't have to prove that I belong.

Free speech assumes that your existence, your humanity and your right to exist are unquestionable – that there is nothing for you to justify or prove. Free speech also means being able to speak as if your perspective were accessible to every listener. In the words of the Vietnamese American author Viet Thanh Nguyen,

> Writers from a minority, write as if you are the majority. Do not explain. Do not cater. Do not translate. Do not apologize. Assume everyone knows what you are talking about, as the majority does. Write with all the privileges of the majority, but with the humility of a minority.
>
> Why write with the humility of a minority? Because humiliated people often do not learn the lesson of humility. That's why the powerless, when they become powerful, often abuse power. Don't become just like the majority. Be better. Wiser. Humble. Yet still confident.[9]

Free speech means emancipating ourselves from a language that doesn't provide for us – by changing it, instead of explaining ourselves, and by using it differently, so that we can *be* in it.

*

'Critical potatoism'[10] is a neologism that references 'critical whiteness', but instead calls white people 'potatoes'. It's a term you probably won't hear on traditional political TV talk shows – but you certainly will when you tune in to *Karakaya Talk*, a programme that has enriched Germany's digital TV landscape since 2018.[11] Its guests and its creator, producer and host, Esra Karakaya, sometimes use terms like this half-jokingly, but mostly organically and sincerely. Terms like 'critical potatoism' or 'Alman' (a Turkish word for Germans) carry within them specific points of view: those of marginalised groups, which otherwise only appear on the scene as objects of observation. What makes the programme different from others, therefore, is not only that it provides a platform for diverse voices, but that they speak without trying to describe and explain their existence. This stance is in itself an emancipatory act. Esra Karakaya does this by engaging with her guests, talking to them as equals and giving their thoughts, personalities and vulnerability room to breathe.

In the first episode she discussed a controversial advert by a big-name confectioner, which showed a model in a hijab. She had invited not just *one* guest who wore a hijab, or even two or three, but *exclusively* women who wore one. This was one of the reasons why none of the guests was under pressure to represent *the* hijab-wearing woman.

Instead, they were all there in their capacity as experienced and knowledgeable individuals.

When I asked Karakaya what the show meant to her, as a space for alternative ways of speaking and languages, she replied:

> The first thing that comes to mind is honesty. I want to exist naturally in a room, just as I am. This is how I speak! I know that, here, no one is above me. I don't depend on anyone. We draw up the framework and the rules – the framework is designed to make us, and me, feel comfortable. I want to be comfortable when I use slang and talk in Kanak. It's about freedom. It's a brilliant feeling, sitting there and hearing people talk in a certain special way, and knowing that you'd never be able to sit there and talk like that [on another show]; they would destroy you, or at the very least pick you apart, look for holes, and take the opportunity to cut you down to size even more. Just knowing that we can do what we want and say what we want is great. It's to do with healing. With freedom and healing.

When I saw the film *Moonlight* in 2016 – which tells the story of a Black, gay man's life in the US – there were many scenes I didn't understand. I didn't have the requisite knowledge, and didn't know enough of the context and references; I am neither Black nor gay nor a man, and don't live in the US. Nevertheless, the film made an impression on me – because it showed me the things I didn't know, and because it explained my own limits to me by telling the story in a way that assumed a certain foreknowledge; the film knew there were things someone like me wouldn't understand, and it was fine with that. However, I only realised this because I normally don't have much of a problem decoding US films. I could easily put myself in the shoes of a white man in the US, and understood many of the cultural references. Why was that? The reason for this is clearly that we've all seen the world from the point of view of white American men millions of times – we are used to seeing women, children, nature, non-whites, other countries, continents and ultimately even ourselves through their eyes. Just as people who live in the countryside are used to seeing the world through the eyes of people who live in cities, women through the eyes of men, poor people through the eyes of wealthy people, and so on.

How would our perception of society change, if we observed and described it exclusively through the eyes of someone living in poverty? How would the stories we tell about ourselves change, and thus society itself?

At this point, someone might say, 'All right, then, let's hear a story from someone else's perspective for a change.' But for there to be change we need a persistent multitude of views. *One* new story – an *exception* – is not enough. We need to see the world from many and completely different perspectives, existing alongside each other as equals.

In the TV series *Derry Girls*, a comedy about a group of Northern Irish friends set during the Troubles in the 1990s, there's a scene where the girls decide to rebel against their school's uniform policy. They want to be allowed to wear their own jackets rather than the school blazer, to express their 'individuality'. However, on the way to school the next morning only one of them, Clare, shows up wearing a denim jacket. She's indignant.

'What's all this? I thought we were going to be individuals this year?'

'Look, I wanted to, Clare, but my Ma wouldn't let me,' says Erin.

'Well, I'm not being individual on me own!' says Clare, and takes off her jacket.[12]

We need millions who speak freely.

I don't have conclusive answers to the questions I ask in this book, but I know that this idea of free speech comes close to being one. We – the exhibits in the Museum of Language – need to stop speaking in order to make ourselves understood, and speak in order to be. Whether or not we are understood, it's when we stop seeing ourselves through other people's eyes that we'll be free.

*

Men are their own reference point, and assume their own supremacy; [...] they then proceed to encode the meanings of society and to enforce their meanings on those who don't share them, so that their supremacy is realised at the expense of women. This process – the double standard – ensures that no matter what they do, men are perceived as better than women.

Dale Spender, For the Record[13]

Inevitably, some will object that if everyone speaks from their point of view, if every story requires a certain foreknowledge and can't be understood by everyone else, people won't be able to understand each other at all. The objection will come from those who aren't accustomed to *not* 'understanding' others – because everyone used to see the world through their eyes. For everyone else, though, the world has always been complicated. They have always spoken more than one language, and have always heard stories in which there were no characters that resembled them. *They can* live in a world where some things are left unexplained, where not everything is adapted to their point of view, where they know that their perspective is just one of many.

If a blonde, blue-eyed white woman attends a friend's Turkish family celebration, a Nigerian wedding, an Indian Henna Night or some other party or event where a white person sticks out, people will often look after her. They might explain the unwritten rules, introduce her to other guests, and make sure that she feels at home and doesn't make any blunders. They aren't merely being hospitable. What lies behind their behaviour is an awareness of difference and of the insufficiency of individual perspective, a knowledge of different ways of life – as well as the experience, which has become habitual, of needing to explain yourself, having to translate your way of life and adapt it to the perspective of the dominant society. On such occasions, it sometimes happens that everyone's attention shifts to the white person and their well-being. Some people act differently in their presence, because they are being 'observed' now, and thus maybe also being evaluated, judged. The white friend becomes a spectator, and therefore doesn't have the opportunity to experience how hard it is when your perspective is in the minority and you are conscious of your own insufficiency. When the situation is reversed, i.e. when I am the only visibly non-white person at an event, people almost always assume that I'll be all right, that I'll work out the rules quickly enough not to blunder. And I am fine with that, because I'm aware of the limits of my knowledge and my perception. It is a skill that we, the others, acquire. It's a gift.

In her essay 'How can white Americans be free?', the film-maker and author Kartina Richardson argues that white norms also rob white people of their individuality. 'How can white people be free to suffer without appearing to forget the violent injustices of the country and the enormous burden that the myth of Whiteness places on the black and brown consciousness?'[14] How can someone who is comparatively privileged express their individual suffering without those on whose oppression this person's privilege was built calling it irrelevant? Richardson knows how absurd it sounds to worry that the suffering of privileged people might not be taken seriously; but her question is important, because it shows that norms imprison even those who profit from them.

One evening after a reading, a white author told a room full of writers of colour, 'You're the future. You actually have something meaningful and relevant to tell.' She didn't say it with envy, but sincerely and full of hope.[15] It reminded me that I had actually thought something similar once, at another reading. That evening, an award-winning German author had just read from her latest book. It was cleverly written; I think it was about numbers and animals. I was spellbound for a few minutes, but grew bored – it didn't have enough urgency for me. Then it was the turn of the Palestinian poet Ghayath Almadhoun, who was born in Damascus and had fled Syria before the war, and now lived in Stockholm. Despite the fact that most of the audience had to have his poetry translated for them, every single one of his sentences had an unbelievable, almost physical, force, and his images – of blood on diamonds, of migrants drowning, of people breathing, floating, dying – stayed with you. Reflecting on the way that immigrants crossing water drown beneath it, but then float when they are dead, he asks why it can't be the other way around – why the water can't lift them when they are still alive. It's a question that has haunted me.

Was the relevance of her art diminished by his art? In a world where her perspective is accepted and his is marginalised, yes; but a different world is possible too, one where they can both coexist as different but equal perspectives, a world where he would be free to muse on trivialities and she could describe her pain without seeming ignorant.

But we don't yet live in such a world. We don't yet live in a social system where everyone's humanity is acknowledged, and where one person's point of view is not seen as a threat to those of other people. Only when we have said goodbye to any claims to sovereignty; only when no one perspective dominates all others, renders all others subordinate and suppresses them; only then can all of us

– regardless of origin, ethnicity, body, religion, sexuality, gender or nationality – speak *freely*. Only then can all of us *be*.

10

A New Way of Speaking

'Would you tell me, please, which way
I ought to walk from here?'
'That depends a good deal on where you
want to get to,' said the Cat.

Lewis Carroll, Alice's Adventures in Wonderland[1]

I have three questions for you: would you, too, like to live in a pluralist society in future? If yes, would you like to enjoy equal rights and be on a par with everyone else? And what does it mean, in practice, to have equal rights and be on a par with everyone else in a pluralist society?

What does it mean to sit at a table together with all those who were previously refused a seat at the table?

The sociologist Aladin El-Mafaalani applies the metaphor of the table to current socio-political conflicts. We talk more about sexism now than we did in the 1960s – but the reason for this is not that things are worse than they were, but that women have become more demanding as they have advanced socially, politically and economically. They want to be treated as *true* equals. They want to be paid equally. They want others to respect them, their bodies, their work and their intellect. Or let's take immigration: according to

El-Mafaalani, the first generation of immigrants didn't sit at the table, but on the floor or at occasional tables. The second generation, their children, some of whom were born or socialised in the new country, gradually claimed their seat at the table, and their share of the meal. The third generation, for its part, wants to decide along with everyone else around the table *what* they are served, and questions the rules that govern proceedings at the table. This generation thus demands and claims more from society – which increases the potential for conflict.[2] He argues that a woman who wears a hijab and works as a cleaner at a school doesn't trigger a debate about fundamental principles. On the other hand, a woman who wears a hijab and wants to teach at a school is considered a problem.[3] According to El-Mafaalani, the paradox is that 'successful integration [...] [raises] the potential for conflict, because inclusion, equal rights and more opportunities to participate lead not to a more homogenous way of life but to heterogenisation, not to greater social harmony and consensus but to more dissonance and renegotiation'; and that a common language is transformed by participation.[4]

When new arrivals join the table but aren't content with what they are served, some people call them impertinent. 'They should be grateful they're allowed to sit at the table at all! If you don't like it here, why don't you go back where you came from?'[5] When you say something like this, you betray a fundamentally racist attitude. According to this attitude, whether or not you belong depends on your fulfilling certain conditions that aren't required of everyone. 'If you want the same rights, you have to behave properly.'

But why? Why should a woman be quietly satisfied and grateful to have been given a leadership job, instead of behaving like a man in the same position and seek to improve and change the structure of the business? Why should a young Black man be quietly satisfied and grateful to be allowed to exist in this country, instead of behaving like young white men and make political demands, critique society and work towards structural change?

Among other things, pluralism means accepting minorities and marginalised groups with all their potential as well as with all their problems – not in order to ignore or romanticise them, but to solve them *together*. Because we need to coexist. The problems aren't *theirs*, they are not *foreign* or *external* problems, but *our* problems. A well-paid male doctor who is originally from Ghana is as much part of this as the alcoholic woman who is originally from Italy; teachers just as much as the unemployed, architects just as much as drug addicts, scientists just as much as criminals, poets just as much as extremists. Not because we approve of unemployment, drug addiction, criminality or extremism, but because we are all responsible for the problems that exist within society. *Everyone's* children are potentially affected by them. It's no use seeing the fight against Islamist extremism as the *sole* responsibility of those who happen to share the same faith; it's no use seeing the fight against right-wing extremism as the *sole* responsibility of those who happen to come from the same neighbourhoods. Of course, the specific circumstances in each case do play a role, but these *others* are neither *solely* responsible for the problem, nor can they solve it on their own. Yes, they are responsible. As is society as a whole. We can only do it together.

'Either let us practice the democracy we are preaching, or shut up,' said the civil rights activist Adam Clayton Powell, Jr. in 1964.[6] If we truly want to live in a pluralist society where everyone has equal rights and is on a par with everyone else, we cannot merely sell the *illusion* of equal rights and plurality.

We can determine whether or not we're dealing with an illusion by asking the following question: who is meant, when someone refers to 'our' children? Do people involved in politics, media and educational institutions – the places where our future is negotiated – talk about certain children as if they were not 'ours', as if they were 'other people's' children? If yes, then we are selling a lazy illusion. Only when 'our children' means *all* children are we one step closer to attaining our ideals.

This conflict between ideals and reality leads to the irritability we can perceive in current discourses on immigration, refugees and integration. We are no longer satisfied with illusions. The social scientist Naika Foroutan writes that we 'are failing in our own demand for an open, enlightened democracy':

The conflict at the core of post-migrant societies focuses only superficially on migration – in reality, the conflict is driven by the negotiation and acceptance of equality as the central promise of modern democracies that see plurality and parity as fundamental principles.[7]

Thus most contemporary conflicts are actually about the transformation of our ideals into reality – ideals that are enshrined in the Universal Declaration of Human Rights, which declares that 'All are equal before the law',[8] in the US Civil Rights Act of 1964 and in the UK's Human Rights Act of 1998, which states that all rights should be secured 'without discrimination on any ground such as sex, race, colour, language, religion, political or other opinion, national or social origin, association with a national minority, property, birth or other status'.[9] Yet discrimination still happens, and people are still being disadvantaged. Every day we witness the distance that separates our reality from our ideals. What can we learn from this? Firstly, that our dissatisfaction is a good sign; it proves that we are able to perceive the discrepancy and understand that we still have a long way to go. Secondly, if we are serious about equal rights, about living peacefully and respectfully alongside each other, about permanence and about justice, we need more than a few tweaks here and there – we need a *proper* culture change.

What does such a culture change look like? Imagine a company that prides itself on its 'inclusivity', and which employs exactly *one* woman with a disability. She is mobile and uses a wheelchair, but there are no ramps in the building, and team excursions always take place at sites that are not accessible. As long as no real culture change happens, people who are employed – or exhibited – here and there in top jobs or other public-facing roles because they are in some way 'different' will remain 'tokens', mere fig leaves for a supposedly inclusive society. Ensuring that everyone can fully participate in society isn't the end of culture change. It is only the beginning. The very first step. A prerequisite.

It's the same in relationships: when you have a new partner, emotional openness is not the goal, but the prerequisite for getting to know the other person – and yourself – better, with everything that it entails, weaknesses and strengths, quirks and flaws. You have to learn to accept and love each other with all your contradictions and complexities. The process inevitably changes you. The same goes for society. But if we want to create a culture of genuine, peaceful coexistence, change is necessary. All of us will have to change. Together.

*

The thought that change is inevitable scares a lot of people. It makes us afraid of *foreigners*, who will change *us*, and afraid that we will lose *ourselves*.

Where does this fear come from? Does it have something to do with the difficulty of acknowledging that those who are described as 'foreigners' are human beings, with equal rights? 'Feminism: the radical notion that women are people', runs a famous quote by the author and feminist activist Marie Shear.[10] Her point is that what is actually radical is the injustice we're meant to uphold, because it affects our *fellow humans*, with whom we'll be walking into the future – one way or another.

What actually scares us is the question of what kind of future we are walking into. What will it look like, how will we shape it? Social change makes everyone anxious, because it means saying goodbye to the old – for the sake of an uncertain future. What would a world look like where no one is discriminated against because of the colour of their skin, their gender, their religion, their class or their sexual orientation? A world where people only take what they actually need, where they consume only as much as the planet can handle? A world where wealth is not created by exploiting and dehumanising others? To be honest, we can't be certain. I don't know a world like that. No one does.

However, it is probably safe to say that a more just society won't simply *happen* of its own accord at some point. The sociologist Erik Olin Wright argues that if 'social and political justice [...] [are] to be our future, it will be brought about by the conscious action of people acting collectively to bring it about'.[11] Once we let go of the notion that ideals have to be realised everywhere at once, we will be free to open up spaces *now* where we can try out utopias 'as best we can', knowing full well that the experiment can only be partially successful.[12] Wright calls these places 'real utopias', and argues that we should divest ourselves of the illusion that we can create perfect institutions once and for all, and then rest for ever more. 'We can never relax,' he writes, because there can be no such thing as a perfect institution that corresponds to every ideal of a just society, and 'no institutional design can ever be perfectly self-correcting'. This requires constant vigilance and continual learning: 'In the end the realization of those ideals will depend on human agency, on the creative willingness of people to participate in making a better world, learning from the inevitable mistakes, and vigorously defending the advances that are made.'[13]

What we need right now are therefore not imposed formulas or easy, simplistic answers, but inclusive and transparent discussions about the future of society. And no, I don't mean TV talk shows, with their orchestrations of polarised opinion and rigid front lines. But new ways of talking to each other and thinking together on the one hand, and on the other hand *different*, future-orientated questions – especially those for which we don't yet have answers.

*

> You must live the questions now. Perhaps one day, in the distant future, you will then gradually, without noticing it, live your way into an answer.
>
> *Rainer Maria Rilke,* Letters to a Young Poet[14]

Whenever we identify a problem, we immediately feel obliged to suggest a solution. I know the impulse well – it has governed my whole life; yet by doing that we leave the problem's deeper, systemic causes unexplored. What if we instead looked at the whole host of problems and injustices that prevail in society, side by side? Might it reveal a different, new picture, one that clarifies their structural relationships?

Since 2018, thousands – by now millions – of young people have been turning their sights on the climate emergency as part of the Fridays for Future movement. They are intent on making the world aware of the full extent of the problem, and refuse to be mollified by political gestures – which is exactly as it should be, for many of those symbolic actions merely plug the holes of what are fundamentally inadequate systems, thereby delaying or even blocking our efforts to fix them. The fact that these young people are now being criticised for 'only' pointing out the problem, without offering a concrete strategic solution, is symptomatic of an age-old attitude: in discussions about social justice, for example, victims of social injustice also often find themselves cast in the role of disruptor. *They* make a nuisance of themselves by identifying injustice. For instance, when Travellers talk about anti-Traveller racism, they are criticised for making their case from the standpoint of the victim. As the journalist Carolin Emcke argues, however, 'people who defend themselves against inequality or exclusion are often compelled to refer to categories that were only created by that exclusion'.[15]

Young people have the power and the duty to question tradition, conventions and convictions. At a Passover Seder, a friend told me that at religious festivals his family would place the children in the middle, surrounded by adults, and in the course of the evening allow them to ask as many questions as they wanted to about faith, God, anything at all. He told me that asking questions keeps children's – and adults' – minds and intellects sharp. Asking the right questions, the important questions, is the real challenge in an age when we're allowing ourselves to be entertained and distracted by absurd questions.

When I once listed examples of injustice during a

panel discussion about feminism, the host interrupted me, saying, 'Okay, and now let's have a few positive things. What's going well?'

It annoyed me. Is it such a bad thing to point out what's going wrong? It is important that we sustain the tension by continuing to identify injustices, so that we can come to understand the structural causes underlying the symptoms – which can be so much harder to grasp – as well as the pattern of discrimination: what links anti-Semitism, anti-Muslim racism, sexism, ableism and so on.

This is exactly what intersectionality demands. The scholar Kimberlé Williams Crenshaw, who introduced the concept in the late 1980s, illustrated the problem using the example of Black women, whose experience of discrimination is characterised by sexism, racism and 'crosscurrents' of both.[16] Long-term success in the fight against discrimination will only be possible if we think about its various forms simultaneously, if we take a few steps back, look at the overall picture and ask ourselves: what do these injustices have in common?

That kind of thinking requires new discursive spaces. But where are they, the spaces where we can think out loud, in public? What alternatives are there to a mode of public debate whereby fixed, and supposedly incontrovertible, positions constantly collide with each other on social media, stages and talk shows, without exploring other options, without any room for doubt, hesitation or thoughtfulness?

Those are the very things we need: hesitation. Doubt. The opportunity to change your mind. The opportunity to question your own position. We need spaces where we can truly think – not in order to show off how brilliant we (believe we) are and how much we (think we) know, but how much we *don't* know and how keen we are to explore, fathom and learn.

What might such spaces look like? How might they facilitate a new way of speaking?

*

It was a liberating moment, when I was invited on stage to discuss global disarmament as part of the Israeli artist, film-maker and photographer Yael Bartana's performance piece *What if Women Ruled the World?* During the discussion I was not *I*, but a fictional character. I didn't have to worry about how other people perceived me. This is what I miss in public discourse: the freedom, the serenity, the intellectual playfulness – the carefree boldness to think big, radically and out loud, while sharing things you yourself haven't yet thought through, and introducing ideas that someone else can then pick up and take further.

But how can communal thinking work, exactly? The quantum physicist and philosopher David Bohm argues that in 'true dialogue' there doesn't have to be a winner:

> Everybody wins if anybody wins. There is a different sort of spirit to it. In a dialogue, there is no attempt to gain points, or to make your particular view prevail. Rather, whenever any mistake is discovered on the part of anybody, everybody gains. It's a situation called

win-win, whereas the other game is win-lose – if I win, you lose. But a dialogue is something more of a common participation, in which we are not playing a game against each other but with each other. In a dialogue, everybody wins.[17]

This requires that all participants forego their claim to authority, and acknowledge their own fallibility. Bohm describes how this allows a new thinking to develop, which builds on the 'development of a common meaning' that is always changing and unfinished:

People are no longer primarily in opposition, nor can they be said to be interacting, rather they are participating in this pool of common meaning which is capable of constant development and change. In this development the group has no pre-established purpose, though at each moment a purpose which is free to change may reveal itself. The group thus begins to engage in a new dynamic relationship in which no speaker is excluded, and in which no particular content is excluded. Thus far we have only begun to explore the possibilities of dialogue in the sense indicated here, but going further along these lines would open up the possibility of transforming not only the relationship between people, but even more, the very nature of consciousness in which these relationships arise.[18]

Yet should our tolerance for our interlocutor's point of view during this act of collective thinking be limitless? The author Robert Jones, Jr. formulated a rule in this regard which is both simple and clear: 'We can disagree and still love each other unless your disagreement is rooted in my oppression and denial of my humanity and right to exist.'[19] We should never sit at a table like that. If we want to think together and out loud, we need rules and boundaries.

Naturally, you can ask whatever questions you like, but does everyone *have to* answer every question they are asked, in any context? People sometimes ask the most absurd things – such as whether I leave my hijab on in the shower. Even if it were possible to answer this question in the context of a private conversation, it absolutely does not belong in a talk show watched by millions of people. Why? Because it confines me, and any other woman who wears a hijab, to the role of an object – and ultimately turns us into an object of ridicule. Do we really have to discuss whether Black people can be good neighbours? The criteria should always be: does the question have any real social relevance, is it constructive, does it somehow take us a step further? Or is it merely intended to create fear and helplessness?

None of these orchestrated discussions unmasks the xenophobia that is propagated by the participants, on the contrary: xenophobia is granted airtime and relevance, and elevated to an *opinion*, while anyone who opposes it has to negotiate the *degree* to which they are dehumanised. And what happens when those committed to opposing xeno-phobia refuse to play the game? Then they are accused of being incapable of discussing things, of being unreason-able and unable to handle diverging *opinions*.

*

When Dale Spender collected the work of other feminists in her book *For the Record*, and thus also *wrote about*, arranged and commented on it, she gave everyone the chance to respond before publication, i.e. within the book itself. As their replies started coming in, Spender began to realise 'that many feminist theorists who have, with the greatest integrity, "come out" with their ideas and explanations, [...] have made themselves vulnerable doing so, only to be scorned for their efforts'. This taught her that

> We simply cannot afford to hit so hard at our sisters so that they withdraw, and determine not to risk themselves again. [...] What painful irony if we perceive our different interpretations as more in need of condemnation than those huge differences which divide us from patriarchal understandings.[20]

Spender is arguing here not that we should abstain from criticism, but that we should be sensitive to the extent, form and type of criticism we dispense. She argues for a well-meaning discourse shaped by exchange, not exclusion.

What a truly collective thinking about our collective future requires more than anything is *goodwill* among those who subscribe to the same fundamental values. Critical thinking doesn't mean elevating ourselves above those whom we criticise. Well-meaning criticism means opening the door to your interlocutor. Criticism does not preclude consent – only that way can we create new trains of thought that are accessible to everyone, even if we don't all agree.

We are only human. We will make mistakes. We will hurt others, and they will hurt us. Yet we'll only be able to succeed as a collective if we don't install each other in fixed positions, if we don't entrench ourselves or others in rigid points of view. We would never have learnt to walk, speak, read or write without making mistakes. It's only through human error that we can come to understand the world, and ourselves.

If we want to enable collective thinking, we have to learn to grant each other the possibility of development, the freedom to become – especially now, in the digital age, where every mistake, folly, moment of weakness or shade of darkness in our process of becoming human will remain for ever discoverable in the digital archive. It's all too easy to reduce someone to the moment when they were at their weakest – just because it happened in public or was made public. It's easy to feel morally superior.

Yet that's how political discourse – online as much as offline – degenerates into a culture of mutual surveillance, whose one ambition seems to be to hunt down other people's mistakes. Critique and scorn are the currency of the digital age: how skilfully can we defame someone's character? How deftly can we shoot someone down online? If, instead, we want to make room for collective thinking, we require patience and goodwill, with regard to ourselves as well as everyone else who shares our aims. Without it, there will never be a space where we can think together publicly.

As yet, we are only *moving towards* a society that is

genuinely fair, inclusive and free from discrimination and extremism. There is no such thing as 'the perfect democrat', 'the committed citizen' or 'the ideal social justice advocate'. No one can fight every hour of every day against every kind of discriminating system, for eco-consciousness, against small- and large-scale violence, against war and injustice in our world. Everything we do is a compromise between our ideals and the reality in which we live.

We can do no other.

'Is there space among the woke for the still-waking?' asks the writer Anand Giridharadas,[21] arguing that political awakening – i.e. wokeness, being aware of injustice and oppression, willing to champion plurality – is a *process*, not a position we can reach and rest in.

Nobody is perfect. Some are more determined than others, some are stronger, or bolder, or simply more privileged in terms of opportunities. No one embodies the ideal. Sometimes it's enough to know that you have tried the impossible, failed, and nevertheless progressed a little further. The feminist author Roxane Gay puts it best in her book *Bad Feminist*:

> I embrace the label of bad feminist because I am human. I am messy. I'm not trying to be an example. [...] I am not trying to say that I have all the answers. I'm not trying to say I'm right. I am just trying [...] to support what I believe in, trying to do some good in this world, trying to make some noise with my writing while also being myself. [...] I would rather be a bad feminist than no feminist at all.[22]

A New Way of Speaking

We need to be aware of our own fallibility. We also need spaces where we can test out the future and practise a new way of speaking: doubtful, thoughtful, questioning, sometimes loudly, sometimes quietly – and always with kindness. This book constitutes a contribution to the search for a new language in which we can all exist as human beings, equally and in all our complexity; and an act of thinking on the path towards turning our ideal of a better society into reality. Or as the philosopher Simone Weil would put it, our attention ought to be 'continually concentrated on the distance there is between what we are and what we love'.[23] I hope it will inspire you to become conscious of the architecture, and thus also the limits, of our speech, thoughts, emotions and lives, and to work on them; to realise that this world, in its current form, is not a just one – however comfortable it may be for some people; and to think about *real* change, even if it occasionally makes things a bit disagreeable, and even if there are more questions than answers.

I hope that it will inspire you to hope, and never to get used to injustice.

I hope that it will inspire you to become aware of your own perspective and limitations, and thus of the kind of place our world could be.

I hope that it will inspire you to participate in building a society in which we truly want to live. Where everyone can speak, and be, on the same terms as everyone else.

Acknowledgements

And one of His signs is the creation of the heavens and
earth, and the diversity of your languages and colours.
There truly are signs in this for those who know.

Surah 30, Verse 22[24]

I am grateful to have been able to write this book, because
it was an opportunity for me to leave behind the familiar,
take several steps back and open myself to a much calmer,
more comprehensive look at the world. It allowed me not
only to take the time to analyse the present, but also to
explore paths into a desirable future. As Kader Abla found
out before I did, the moment she spoke she became visible. As Grada Kilomba realised, the moment she wrote
her book she turned from an object into a subject.

When the book was published in German, I was repeatedly asked in interviews to explain my feelings towards
English, German, Turkish and Arabic, and the attributes I
valued in these languages (referring to what I say in Chapter
2, that 'for me, Turkish is the language of love and melancholy. Arabic is a mystical, spiritual melody. German is the
language of intellect and longing. English is the language
of freedom'). To my amazement, I was surprised by this
question. For I was no longer the person I was when I wrote
those words. These different languages, each of which had

provided a home for a different facet of my being, were no longer hermetically sealed off from one another. I no longer felt lost among them, or living with the bitter realisation that no matter what language I was operating in, I would always be missing the other facets – that I could not exist in completeness in any of the languages I spoke. The longing to be at home in a language that did not envision me as a speaker, but merely as someone being spoken about, had disappeared. What changed? It was writing this book, and reading about how James Baldwin fought with the English language (see Chapter 2) and made it his own. Baldwin transformed the English language to suit his own experience. He took it upon himself to edit it. Not as a guest, but as a host. The process of researching my book, writing it, publishing it, and the discourse around it changed everything. Now I knew how I would make language my home. Because being at home in a language is just like being at home in a society, a country, a house, a room. Only when you are no longer a guest, but a host, are you at home there. When you no longer have to ask permission, when you move tentatively and carefully through the building of language, when you no longer have the feeling of being too much but feel just right, then you are at home. You are at home when you no longer need to be called upon to speak but can speak up for yourself. When you tear down those oppressive walls – the words that dehumanise people – and unlock new, rich spaces, expanding them with words that open up the world, new ways of seeing. When you install doors and windows – and leave them wide open. When you continually open yourself to new, different, critical perspectives. When you

Acknowledgements

introduce into a language all the facets and nuances that were previously hidden from it. Then you are at home – in a language, a room, a building, a society, a city, a country. You are at home when you speak and write not to explain yourself, but to be; not to make yourself understood, but to understand the world. When you learn to look at the world that lies beyond the field of vision not only of the powerful, but of all others. When you learn to speak not only to the powerful, but to everyone else.

And so, thank you to all of you who came before me and paved the way for me with your knowledge, your discoveries, your battles, your lives and the many words you have created to widen our perception of the world, for a better future. I am grateful to have been able to get to know you through your books and your work. When I read what you have written, I am humbled and delighted to have the chance to join in the conversation of your thoughts, in the hope that I might bring them a little closer to each other.

Thank you to all of you who were by my side throughout the time I spent writing this book – with your thoughts, advice, intellect and/or friendship: Şeyma Preukschas, Emilia Roig, Michael Seemann, Teresa Bücker, Rea Mahrous, Canan Bayram, Meltem Kulaçatan, Sookee, Mareice Kaiser, Lann Hornscheidt, Bahar Aslan, Sertaç Sehlikoğlu, Anne Wizorek, Hatice Akyün, Naika Foroutan, Margarete Stokowski, Annina Loets, Marie Meimberg, Anja Saleh, Christoph Rauscher, Milena Glimbowski, Mithu Sanyal, Tupoka Ogette, Tsepo Bollwinkel, Anatol Stefanowitsch, Max Czollek and Bernd Ulrich. For the English translation: first and foremost, thank you to my editor Louisa Dunnigan for her trust and vision; to the incredibly talented translator Gesche Ipsen for bringing this book to life in yet another language; to Basil Wright for a thoughtful sensitivity read; and to my friend Aina Khan for helping to adapt these thoughts to a new audience.

Thank you to all of you who shared your thoughts with me for the purpose of this book (you are priceless!), the members of various chat groups (among them 'allerbeste') and the guests and musicians who attended our inspirational 'story nights', where I was fortunate to be able to repeatedly experience a new way of speaking, and the future before it happens.

Thank you to the editors of *Bref* magazine, for helping me to discover my voice; to the Alfred Toepfer and Roger Willemsen foundations, for providing me with wonderful places to write, where I found inspiration and peace; and to my companions in that shack out in the sticks, Alice Hasters and Ronja von Wurmb-Seibel. Thanks also to the German Cultural Academy Tarabya in Istanbul for allowing me to edit this translation while looking at the most beautiful view, the Bosporus.

Thank you to my agent, Franziska Günther, and to my publishing house, Hanser Berlin, for their faith and encouragement, especially to my publisher, editor and intellectual midwife Karsten Kredel. Thank you for your ever-critical, ever-vigilant mind, with whose help I could grow. Thank you to my friend Nes Kapucu for the cover of the German edition of this book – what talent! And thank you to Julia Obermann, who always has my back.

Thank you to my parents, İbrahim and Ayşe. Bana

aşıladığınız güvenle, bulunduğum her yere ve çevremdeki her insana tereddüt etmeden sevgiyle yaklaşabildim. Bana bir ana babanın çocuğuna verebileceği en güzel hediyeleri verdiniz, bir ömürlük dost ve yoldaşlarım, kardeşlerimi hayatıma kattınız. Sorumluluk sahibi bir birey, evlat, abla ve kardeş olmayı ve en önemlisi kulluğu öğrettiniz. Düşeni kaldırmanın bir sorumluluk olduğunu, gayretin zaferden evla olduğunu öğrettiniz. Bugün durduğum yerden geriye baktığımda, yaşadıklarımda, hissettiklerimde ve sahip olduğum her şeyde beni ben yapan izlerinizi görüyorum. Umarım sizlere duyduğum minneti hayırlı bir evlat olarak göstermek Allah'ın izniyle nasip olur.

Thank you to my grandfather Mehmet, with whom my family's new life in Germany began. Babaannem ve bizler seni çok özlüyoruz. Mekanın cennet olsun, dedeciğim.

Thank you to Ali, the man by my side. Without you, this book would not exist. Thank you for your heart, your intellect and your faith – in me, in us, and in what it means to be human in this world. Thank you for your love; for loving me and the greatest little blessing in our lives.

I thank you, little person. When you were born my eyes were opened anew, and with you I have been able to reopen them again and again ever since. May the words that your grandfather whispered into your ear be your life-long companion.

And: *Hamdulillah*.

Kübra Gümüşay,
Hamburg, October 2019 and Istanbul, August 2021

Notes

1. When I first read these words by the Persian poet Jalāl ad-Dīn Mohammad Rūmī, I tried to find the Persian original – but to no avail. Now I know why: they are a loose paraphrase by Coleman Barks. Barks does not read or speak Persian, and has been criticised for knowingly erasing references to Islam in his 'interpretations'. Knowing this might affect how we read these lines.
2. Simone Weil, *Selected Essays, 1934–1943: Historical, Political, and Moral Writings* (Eugene, OR: Wipf and Stock Publishers, 2015), p. 26.

1. The Power of Language
1. The word *yakamoz* actually comes from the Greek word *διακαμός* (*diakamós*). In scientific terms, *yakamoz* is a 'phosphorescence in the sea due to bioluminescent dinoflagellates'. See https://en.wiktionary.org/wiki/yakamoz.
2. The Turkish author Elif Şafak describes *gurbet* as an invisible splinter on the tip of your finger, under the skin. She writes: 'You try to remove it – in vain. You try to show it to someone – also in vain. It becomes your flesh, your bones, part of your body. A limb that you can no longer remove, no matter how unfamiliar it is to you, how alien.' Elif Şafak, 'Gurbet', *Haberturk*, 26 November 2011, https://www.haberturk.com/yazarlar/elif-safak/679900-gurbet. (Where no details of an extant English translation are listed, the translation is mine. – GI.)
3. Wilhelm von Humboldt, *Schriften zur Sprachphilosophie* ('Writings on the Philosophy of Language'), vol. 3 (Stuttgart: Klett-Cotta, 1963), p. 224.
4. Holden Härtl, 'Linguistische Relativität und die

"Sprache-und-Denken"-Debatte: Implikationen, Probleme und mögliche Lösungen aus Sicht der kognitionswissenschaftlichen Linguistik' ('Linguistic relativity and the debate about language and thought: Implications, problems and possible solutions from cognitive linguistics'), *Zeitschrift für Angewandte Sprachwissenschaft* 51 (2009), pp. 45–81, https://tinyurl.com/yakov3en.

5. As a matter of fact, 'many' is an imprecise translation of the Pirahã word, which literally means 'to bring together'. See Claire Cameron, '5 Languages That Could Change the Way You See the World', *Nautilus*, 3 May 2015, http://nautil.us/blog/5-languages-that-could-change-the-way-you-see-the-world.

6. They have no terms for 'all', 'every', 'most', 'some', or such. Pirahã is not the only language that does not have words for numbers, but according to Everett the Pirahã are the only people unable to acquire numbers in other languages; Everett and his wife spent years trying to teach them the Portuguese words for the numbers one to ten. The fact that the Pirahã have largely managed to keep outside influence at bay, despite decades of attempts to convert them to Christianity, and despite government interference and regulation, is impressive. See John Colapinto, 'The interpreter: Has a remote Amazonian tribe upended our understanding of language?', *The New Yorker*, 9 April 2007, https://www.newyorker.com/magazine/2007/04/16/the-interpreter-2.

7. Patrick Barkham, 'The power of speech', *The Guardian*, 10 November 2008, https://www.theguardian.com/world/2008/nov/10/daniel-everett-amazon.

8. Daniel Everett, *Don't Sleep, There are Snakes: Life and Language in the Amazonian Jungle* (London: Profile, 2009), pp. 129 and 132.

9. The inscription is above the Garrick pub in Montgomery Street.

10. Kathrin Sperling, 'Geschlechtslose Fräulein, bärtige Schlüssel und weibliche Monde – beeinflusst das grammatische Geschlecht von Wörtern unsere Weltsicht?' ('Ungendered

girls, bearded keys and female moons – does the grammatical gender of words affect our world view?'), *Babbel Magazin*, 25 February 2016, https://de.babbel.com/de/magazine/grammatisches-geschlecht-und-weltsicht.

11. 'Lost in translation: The power of language to shape how we view the world', *Hidden Brain* (Podcast), 29 January 2018, https://www.npr.org/transcripts/581657754.

12. In *Exit Gender* (Berlin: w_orten & meer, 2019), Lann Hornscheidt and Lio Oppenländer show that even in highly gendered languages like German, it is possible to tell stories without mentioning the gender of the people involved.

13. The social scientist Stephen Levinson was the first Western researcher to observe this, and his work significantly contributed to bringing the hypothesis of linguistic relativity to the fore in academic discourse – see Stephen Levinson, 'Language and cognition: The cognitive consequences of spatial description in Guugu Yimithirr', *Journal of Linguistic Anthropology* 7(1) (1997), pp. 98–131, https://pdfs.semanticscholar.org/400c/4086205ebbfacf938478d5b73ea9 eb4b052a.pdf. See also Caleb Everett, *Linguistic Relativity: Evidence Across Languages and Cognitive Domains* (Berlin and Boston: De Gruyter, 2013), p. 20.

14. 'Lost in translation', *Hidden Brain*, 29 January 2018.

15. Ibid.

16. Annabell Preussler, 'Über die Notwendigkeit des (geschlechter)gerechten Ausdrucks' ('Why we need gender-neutral terms'), *maDonna* 1, http://www.gleichstellung.tu-dortmund.de/cms/de/Professor_innen/Geschlechtergerechte_Sprache/__ber_die_Notwendigkeit_des_geschlechtergerechten_Ausdrucks.pdf.

17. Of course, this is a heteronormative answer. The boy could just as easily be the son of a gay couple – a child could thus have two fathers, or indeed one 'biological' and one 'social' father; or this person could just be another parent, neither father nor mother, but just a parent, non-binary.

18. Caroline Criado Perez, *Invisible Women: Exposing Data Bias in a World Designed for Men* (London: Vintage, 2020), p. 6.

19. Monika Dittrich, 'Die Genderfrage im Rechtschreibrat'
   ('The gender question and the Council for German
   Orthography'), Deutschlandfunk, 15 November 2018,
   https://www.deutschlandfunk.de/er-sie-die-genderfrage-im-
   rechtschreibrat.724.de.html?dram:article_id=433109.

20. Dagmar Stahlberg, Sabine Sczesny and Friederike Braun,
   'Name your favorite musician: Effects of masculine generics
   and of their alternatives in German', *Journal of Language
   and Social Psychology* 20(4) (2001), pp. 464–69. See also
   Karin Kusterle, *Die Macht von Sprachformen* ('The Power
   of Linguistic Forms') (Frankfurt am Main, Brandes & Apsel,
   2011).

21. Is there less sexism and less sexist violence in Turkey because
   the grammatical structure of its language is mostly gender-
   neutral ? No – Turkey's femicide rate is among the highest
   in the world, despite its grammar. However, language is just
   one factor; others include media images, film, art, culture,
   the judiciary and the executive, traditional political power
   structures, the economy, educational institutions, religious
   institutions, etc. The patriarchy won't end with language
   reform; but it won't end without it, either.

22. That's why Lann Hornscheidt, from the Centre for
   Transdisciplinary Gender Studies at the Humboldt University
   in Berlin, proposes the use of the -x suffix (as in e.g. 'Latinx')
   'whenever the question whether the person you mean is
   female, male or trans plays no role in the context, or ought
   to play no role'. See the Humboldt University's 'Feministisch
   Sprachhandeln' ('feminist language performance') working
   group's paper 'Was tun? Sprachhandeln – aber wie?
   W_Ortungen statt Tatenlosigkeit' ('What to do? Perform
   language – but how? Word orientation instead of apathy'),
   2014 (2nd edn, 2015), p. 22, http://feministisch-sprachhandeln.
   org/wp-content/uploads/2015/04/sprachleitfaden_zweite_
   auflage.pdf. Hornscheidt's proposal was controversial and
   much discussed in German media, and resulted in smear
   campaigns and threats from right-wingers. But the more I
   think about it, the more it's clear to me that – whether you

use the -x suffix or something else – a path leading towards
a language that doesn't immediately assign a gender identity
to people is the right one to take. Hornscheidt's proposal
is merely a way of saying, 'To me, your gender identity
is (for now) irrelevant – or at any rate not important.' In
Exit Gender, Lann Hornscheidt and Lio Oppenländer also
propose that we begin statements with the words 'The person
who [teaches, sings, rides a bike …]'. The person comes first,
and everything else is merely additional information that
does not represent someone's essence. See Hornscheidt und
Oppenländer, op. cit.

23. Ludwig Wittgenstein, *Tractatus Logico-Philosophicus*,
trans. D. F. Pears and B. F. McGuinness (London: Routledge
Classics, 2001), p. 68.
24. David Foster Wallace, Kenyon College Commencement
Speech, 2005, http://bulletin-archive.kenyon.edu/x4280.html.
25. George Steiner, 'The Hollow Miracle', in *George Steiner: A
Reader* (Oxford: OUP, 1984), p. 219.
26. Ibid., p. 207, n. 1.

2. Between Languages

1. Jhumpa Lahiri, 'I am, in Italian, a tougher, freer writer', *The
Guardian*, 31 January 2016, https://www.theguardian.
com/books/2016/jan/31/jhumpa-lahiri-in-other-words-
italian-language.
2. Ibid.
3. Navid Kermani, 'Ich erlebe Mehrsprachigkeit als einen großen
Reichtum' ('In my experience, speaking several languages is a
great asset'), Goethe-Institut, http://www.goethe.de/lhr/prj/
mac/msp/de2391179.htm.
4. Elif Şafak, 'Writing in English brings me closer to
Turkey', *British Council Voices Magazine*, 19 November
2014, https://www.britishcouncil.org/voices-magazine/
elif-shafak-writing-english-brings-me-closer-turkey.
5. Emine Sevgi Özdamar, *The Bridge of the Golden Horn*
(London: Serpent's Tail, 1998).
6. The Swiss linguist Marie José-Kolly argues that 'if someone

has a foreign accent, native speakers subconsciously draw certain conclusions about their education, social status, intelligence, and even their character'. Marie-José Kolly, 'Weshalb hat man (noch) einen Akzent? Eine Untersuchung im Schnittfeld von Akzent und Einstellung bei Schweizer Dialektsprechern' ('Why do we (still) have accents? Examining the intersection between accent and attitude among speakers of the Swiss dialect'), *Linguistik Online* 50, no. 6 (November 2011), https://doi.org/10.13092/lo.50.319.

7. *Universal Declaration of Linguistic Rights*, World Conference for Linguistic Rights, Article 13.2 (June 1996), https://pen-international.org/app/uploads/drets_culturals389.pdf.

8. Dave Burke, 'Princess Charlotte can already speak two languages – at age TWO', *Daily Mirror*, 13 January 2018, https://www.mirror.co.uk/news/uk-news/princess-charlotte-can-already-speak-11848448.

9. In the event, I won a work experience placement at the paediatric clinic. When Turkish mothers came in with their children and asked me to translate for them, I was sent into a room in the back. In the clinic, too, I wasn't supposed to speak Turkish.

10. Leyla Zana was released from prison early thanks to pressure from the EU, which was in the middle of negotiating Turkey's EU membership. See Alexander Isele, 'Kämpferin – Personalie: Die kurdische Politikerin Leyla Zana droht mit Hungerstreik' ('Fighter – Profile: The Kurdish politician Leyla Zana threatens to go on hunger strike'), *Neues Deutschland*, 14 September 2015, https://www.neues-deutschland.de/artikel/984363.kaempferin.html. Twenty-four years after the 1991 event, in November 2015, Leyla Zana was re-elected to the Turkish parliament, this time for the HDP (People's Democratic Party). She largely swore her oath in Turkish, but instead of the 'Turkish people' she referred to the 'people of Turkey', to highlight that not all of Turkey's population is 'Turkish'. This, too, caused controversy. See Reuters, 'Once-jailed lawmaker again uses Kurdish in Turkey's parliament', https://www.reuters.com/article/idUSKCN0T627T20151117.

She was stripped of her voting rights and, in 2018, of her delegate status. See Reuters, 'Turkish parliament strips pro-Kurdish lawmaker of her status', https://www.reuters.com/article/us-turkey-kurds-parliament-idUSKBN1F02XD.

11. Bejan Matur, *Dağın Ardına Bakmak* ('Looking Beyond the Mountain') (Istanbul: Timaş Yayınları, 2011), p. 89.

12. 'I stumbled upon it in a book by the Anishinaabe ethnobotanist Keewaydinoquay, in a treatise on the traditional uses of fungi by our people. Puhpowee, she explained, translates as "the force which causes mushrooms to push up from the earth overnight."' Robin Kimmerer, *Braiding Sweetgrass* (London: Penguin, 2020), p. 49.

13. Robin Kimmerer, 'Nature needs a new pronoun: To stop the age of extinction, let's start by ditching "it"', *Yes!*, 30 March 2015, https://www.yesmagazine.org/issue/together-earth/2015/03/30/alternative-grammar-a-new-language-of-kinship.

14. Interview with Krista Tippett, 'Robin Wall Kimmerer: The intelligence of plants', On Being, 26 July 2021, transcript, https://onbeing.org/programs/robin-wall-kimmerer-the-intelligence-of-plants/#transcript

15. Robin Kimmerer, *Braiding Sweetgrass* (London: Penguin, 2020), p. 50.

16. Kurt Tucholsky, *Sprache ist eine Waffe. Sprachglossen* ('Language Is a Weapon: Linguistic Asides') (Hamburg: Rowohlt, 1989), p. 48 ff.

17. Colm Tóibín, 'The Henry James of Harlem: James Baldwin's struggles', *The Guardian*, 14 September 2001, https://www.theguardian.com/books/2001/sep/14/jamesbaldwin.

18. James Baldwin, *The Cross of Redemption: Uncollected Writings* (New York: Pantheon, 2011), p. 67.

3. The Political Gap

1. Jacques Derrida, *Monolingualism of the Other, or: The Prosthesis of Origin*, trans. Patrick Mensah (Stanford University Press, 1998), p. 2.

2. 'For something to be an injustice, it must be harmful

but also wrongful, whether because discriminatory or because otherwise unfair. In the present example, harasser and harassee alike are cognitively handicapped by the hermeneutical lacuna – neither has a proper understanding of how he is treating her – but the harasser's cognitive disablement is not a significant disadvantage to him [...] [while] without that understanding she is left deeply troubled, confused, and isolated, not to mention vulnerable to continued harassment. Her hermeneutical disadvantage renders her unable to make sense of her ongoing mistreatment, and this in turn prevents her from protesting it, let alone securing effective measures to stop it.' Miranda Fricker, *Epistemic Injustice: Power and the Ethics of Knowing* (Oxford: OUP, 2007), p. 151.

3. Betty Friedan does not explicitly describe these women as white, but I think it is important to highlight them as such, because working women, women of colour and female immigrants in the US experienced very different realities, in that their lives were affected by additional factors, e.g. racial segregation.

4. Betty Friedan, *The Feminine Mystique* (London: Penguin, 2010), p. 1.

5. Ibid., p. 9.

6. Dale Spender, *For the Record: Making and Meaning of Feminist Knowledge* (London: The Women's Press, 1985), p. 10.

7. Robert Habeck, *Wer wir sein könnten: Warum unsere Demokratie eine offene und vielfältige Sprache braucht* ('Who We Might Be: Why Democracy Needs an Open and Diverse Language') (Cologne: Kiepenheuer & Witsch), p. 125 ff.

8. The author and activist Tupoka Ogette argues that the N-word 'is white people's alien designation for Black people. The word cannot be uncoupled from its racist etymology. The term also refers to the skin colour of people, and accordingly constructs an identity based on the pigmentation of people.' Tupoka Ogette, *exit RACISM: rassismuskritisch denken lernen* ('Exit RACISM: How to Think Raciocritically')

(Münster: Unrast, 2017), p. 75. It's also important to note that there is a discussion taking place about the reclamation of the word by Black people; but what is certain in all contexts is that it is never appropriate for someone who is not Black to use the word. The writer Ta-Nehisi Coates says that 'if you could choose one word to represent the centuries of bondage, the decades of terrorism, the long days of mass rape, the totality of white violence that birthed the Black race in America', it would be the N-word; but also 'that such a seemingly hateful word should return as a marker of nationhood and community confounds our very notions of power'. He writes that this word is 'the border, the signpost that reminds us that the old crimes don't disappear. It tells white people that, for all their guns and all their gold, there will always be places they can never go.' See https://www. nytimes.com/2013/11/24/opinion/sunday/coates-in-defense-of-a-loaded-word.html.

9. 'The insistence on *one* view not only leaves out a great deal (and is therefore partial and inaccurate), it assumes considerable privilege for those whose view it happens to be. They are in the privileged position of knowing "everything": their bias, their limitations, become the yardstick by which all else is measured, and if they have not been exposed to a particular experience – in the way that whites in Western society have not been exposed to the receiving end of racist abuse, the employed have not been exposed to redundancy, men have not been exposed to the everyday routine of the housewife – then such experience can be deemed not to exist: it is *un*real.' *For the Record*, pp. 10–11.

10. The activist Tarana Burke had already used 'Me Too' back in 2006, as a keyword for her Myspace page which tackled the subject of sexual violence against women. It went viral when the actor Alyssa Milano took it up in 2017.

11. This and the subsequent posts were published on Twitter in September 2013.

12. The term 'everyday racism' has since been rightly criticised as

trivialising, and some have suggested that the term 'racism in everyday life' should be used instead.

13. The campaign was initiated by the Australian writer Benjamin Law: 'To celebrate the Coalition tampering with the RDA on #HarmonyDay, let's share stories of racism with hashtag #FreedomOfSpeech. I'll start.' See https://twitter.com/mrbenjaminlaw/status/844020354448211968

14. The two incidents that sparked this campaign were Fox News commentator Bill O'Reilly's racist remarks about US Congresswoman Maxine Waters's hair, and White House Press Secretary Sean Spicer's disrespectful treatment of the veteran journalist April Ryan. In an interview with *Mashable*, activist Brittany Packnett, who kicked off the hashtag campaign, says she started #BlackWomenAtWork 'so people don't think this is rare [...]. It isn't new. It is the daily experience of Black women in the workplace – at all levels – laid bare for the public to finally see with naked eyes [...]. These women at least deserve respect as humans, let alone as professionals. They received neither. It is absolutely unacceptable. They deserve the respect that their humanity, their accomplishments, and their work demands.' See Rachel Thompson, '#BlackWomenAtWork hashtag uncovers the everyday racism black women face at work', *Mashable*, 29 March 2017, https://mashable.com/article/black-women-at-work-hashtag.

15. Andrea Cheong, '"I've experienced the insidious chill of casual racism": Why the #StopAsianHate hashtag is so important', British *Vogue*, 19 February 2021, https://www.vogue.co.uk/arts-and-lifestyle/article/stop-asian-hate-hashtag.

16. I say 'yet another opportunity', because #SchauHin was by no means the start of discussions on racism in Germany. For decades, organisations and activists have paved the way with their books and otherwise intellectual, scholarly or artistic work, to make racism in its everyday, normalised form recognisable and nameable. But we have to continually fill terms anew with meaning. Those who have laid the groundwork for increased awareness about these issues

are too numerous to list, but here are a few examples: organisations such as ADEFRA e.V., ISD e.V. or Der Braune Mob e.V., as well as figures such as May Ayim, Grada Kilomba, Dagmar Schultz, Peggy Piesche, Noah Sow, Mutlu Ergün Hamaz, Fatima El-Tayeb, Sharon Dodua Otoo, Tupoka Ogette, Joshua Kwesi Aikins, Maureen Maisha Eggers, among countless others.

17. https://twitter.com/mrbenjaminlaw/
   status/844020449990262784
18. https://twitter.com/squig_/status/844031106580013058
19. https://twitter.com/NyashaJunior/status/846848921670365184
20. https://twitter.com/LisaCraddock1/
   status/846907645911019521
21. As Dale Spender wrote with regard to the suffragettes, 'When women acted together and validated each other's actions, men had little choice but to change their minds – marginally, anyway. For centuries men may have been checking with each other and confirming the accuracy and adequacy of their descriptions and explanations of the world – and woman – and without any consultation with women. [...] [When] women took the initiative[,] men were obliged to react.' Dale Spender, *Man Made Language* (London: Pandora Press, 1998), pp. 3–4.
22. Probably inspired by the following words of Luxemburg's in *The Mass Strike, the Political Party and the Trade Unions*, Chapter 3, 'Development of the Mass Strike Movement in Russia': '[T]his awakening of class feeling expressed itself forthwith in the circumstances that the proletarian mass, counted by millions, quite suddenly and sharply came to realise how intolerable was that social and economic existence which they had patiently endured for decades in the chains of capitalism. Thereupon, there began a spontaneous general shaking of and tugging at these chains.' Trans. Patrick Lavin (Detroit: Marxist Educational Society, 1925), https://www.marxists.org/archive/luxemburg/1906/mass-strike.
23. Niall McCarthy 'Lone Wolf Terrorism: Majority Of Offenders Are White', *Statista*, 14 November

2019, https://www.statista.com/chart/19968/
the-race-ethnicity-of-lone-offender-terrorists/.

24. Thanks to her intervention, things ended on a hopeful note: 'Tears came to her eyes. *You're right. It's not fair. I'm embarrassed now, but I don't know what to do about it. I just have this bad feeling.*' See https://www.facebook.com/EOTO. eV/posts/2273914666058350.

25. Twitter, 12 June 2015, https://twitter.com/DrMayaAngelou/status/609390085604311040.

26. Grada Kilomba, *Plantation Memories: Episodes of Everyday Racism* (Münster: Unrast Verlag, 2010), p. 28.

27. Caroline Criado Perez, *Invisible Women*, p. 23.

28. Paul Celan, *Eingedunkelt und Gedichte aus dem Umkreis von Eingedunkelt* (Frankfurt am Main: Suhrkamp, 1991), p. 41.

29. Semra Ertan, 'Mein Name ist Ausländer' ('My name is Foreigner'), quoted in Cana Bilir-Meier's 'Nachdenken über das Archiv – Notizen zu Semra Ertan' ('Thoughts about the archive – notes on Semra Ertan'), http://www.canabilirmeier. com/wp-content/uploads/2015/07/Nachdenken-über-das-Archiv---Notizen-zu-Semra-Ertan.pdf. The artist Cana Bilir-Meier is Semra Ertan's niece.

30. See https://vimeo.com/90241760 (5:56).

31. *Hamburger Abendblatt*, 'Erschütternde Verzweiflungstat einer Türkin' ('A Turkish woman's devastating act of desperation'), 1 June 1982, https://web.archive.org/web/20140728185642/http://www.abendblatt.de/archiv/article.php?xmlurl=/ha/1982/xml/19820601xml/habxm1820406_7026.xml.

4. Individuality Is a Privilege

1. Kartina Richardson, 'How can white Americans be free?', *Salon*, 25 April 2013, https://www.salon.com/2013/04/25/how_can_white_americans_be_free/.

2. Vinda Gouma, 'Ich bin die Flüchtlinge!' ('I am the refugees!'), *Der Tagesspiegel*, 28 January 2019, https://www.tagesspiegel.de/gesellschaft/lesermeinung-ich-bin-diefluechtlinge/23917406.html.

3. Ibid.

4. Sara Yasin, 'Muslims shouldn't have to be "good" to be granted human rights', *BuzzFeed*, 21 February 2017, https://www.buzzfeednews.com/article/sarayasin/muslims-shouldnt-have-to-be-good-to-be-granted-human-rights.

5. In 1959, Frantz Fanon, the prominent French thinker and postcolonial theorist, described the aggression and irritation triggered by Muslim women, in particular when they are dressed in a way that resists the curious gaze of those who label them: 'This woman who sees without being seen frustrates the colonizer. There is no reciprocity. She does not yield herself, does not give herself, does not offer herself. The Algerian has an attitude toward the Algerian woman which is on the whole clear. He does not see her. There is even a permanent intention not to perceive the feminine profile, not to pay attention to women. In the case of the Algerian, therefore, there is not, in the street or on a road, that behavior characterizing a sexual encounter that is described in terms of the glance, of the physical bearing, the muscular tension, the signs of disturbance to which the phenomenology of encounters has accustomed us. The European faced with an Algerian woman wants to see. He reacts in an aggressive way before this limitation of his perception. [...] Aggressiveness comes to light [...] in structurally ambivalent attitudes and in the dream material that can be revealed in the European, whether he is normal or suffers from neuropathological disturbances.' Frantz Fanon, *A Dying Colonialism*, trans. Haakan Chevalier (New York: Grove Press, 1994), p. 44.

6. *Plantation Memories*, p. 143.

7. Sheila Rowbotham, *Woman's Consciousness, Man's World* (London: Verso, 2015), p. 32.

8. Naturally, I could consider myself lucky to be able to be the 'hijab-lady' in those situations: to be allowed to represent an entire world religion, indeed, to have the luxury to speak in the name of millions of people without first seeking their permission, without having been selected or elected by them – better still, without their being able to deselect me – simply because it's what media logic demands, because our society

doesn't want to have to deal with complexity, because the public media would like there to be a single person who can represent an entire religion, group of people, country or continent. Sure, you could say that I ought to be grateful for the opportunity to fill this privileged role; but I believe that there is something fundamentally wrong with a system that makes these kinds of dehumanising demands. And I don't plan on playing along.

9. In the summer of 2021, the EU Court of Justice ruled that headscarves can be banned at work 'under certain conditions'. See 'EU court rules headscarves can be banned at work "under certain conditions"', Sky News, 15 July 2021, https://news.sky.com/story/eu-court-rules-headscarves-can-be-banned-at-work-under-certain-conditions-12356521.

10. The journalist Myriam François has documented the experiences of three women in France who wear the hijab. Their accounts are an important demonstration of the impact of these bans. See Myriam François, '"I felt violated by the demand to undress": Three Muslim women on France's hostility to the hijab', *The Guardian*, 27 July 2021, https://www.theguardian.com/world/2021/jul/27/i-felt-violated-by-the-demand-to-undress-three-muslim-women-on-frances-hostility-to-the-hijab.

11. 'Berlin teacher headscarf ban is illegal, rules top court', *Deutsche Welle*, https://www.dw.com/en/berlin-teacher-headscarf-ban-is-illegal-rules-top-court/a-54722770 .

12. If I felt like it, and if I felt that you were actually curious – on a human level – I would give you an explanation, but I've only rarely had that feeling from strangers; I get it more often from people who have known me for a long time, from my friends. Intimate questions like that seem much more appropriate coming from them.

13. There are at least as many reasons why women take off the hijab as why they wear it. There are women who no longer want to, like to or can believe; women who no longer want to be associated with the religious community; women who never wanted to wear one in the first place,

and finally managed to create structures in which they are no longer compelled to; women who see no religious foundation for wearing a hijab; women no longer willing to tolerate sexist, patriarchal structures, who reject the sexist instrumentalisation of the hijab – these are just some of the many, many reasons. So you mustn't take the reason named here to be *the* reason, i.e. turn *one* perspective into a general truth.

14. Martin Buber, *I and Thou*, trans. Ronald Gregor Smith (New York: Scribner, 2000), p. 126.

5. **Worthless Knowledge**

1. Rux Martin, 'Truth, power, self: An interview with Michel Foucault, October 25, 1982', in Luther H. Martin, Huck Gutman and Patrick H. Hutton (eds), *Technologies of the Self: A Seminar with Michel Foucault* (Amherst, MA: University of Massachusetts Press, 1988), p. 9.

2. John Bargh, *Before You Know It: The Unconscious Reasons We Do What We Do* (London: Windmill, 2018), pp. 84–90.

3. One organisation working towards raising awareness of this is the US-based Heart initiative, as part of which Muslim women educate Muslim communities about topics related to sexuality and health, and even address controversial subjects such as abuse by clerics – see, for instance, Nadiah Mohajir, 'Working toward community accountability', Heart, https://hearttogrow.org/?sfid=3131&_sf_s=working%20toward%20community%20accountability. To expose sexism in Muslim communities without reproducing the xenophobic stereotype of the Muslim man is a tough undertaking, but Heart and other programmes and individuals have taken on the challenge – often at a high personal cost.

4. Roxanne A. Donovan und Lindsey M. West, 'Stress and mental health: Moderating role of the Strong Black Woman stereotype', *Journal of Black Psychology* 41(4) (2015), pp. 384–96.

5. Kelly M. Hoffman et al., 'Racial bias in pain assessment and treatment recommendations, and false beliefs about

biological differences between blacks and whites', *Proceedings of the National Academy of Sciences*, April 2016, 113(16), pp. 4296–301.

6. 'Weak Black Women: Official Music Video – The Rundown with Robin Thede', https://www.youtube.com/watch?v=yUswFJ6q_5Q.

7. Max Czollek, *Desintegriert euch!* ('Deintegrate yourselves!') (Munich: Carl Hanser, 2018), p. 192.

8. Quoted by Shermin Langhoff, artistic director of Berlin's Gorki Theatre, in an interview with the *Tagesspiegel*'s Patrick Fildermann. See 'Die Lage in der Türkei verfinstert sich täglich' ('The situation in Turkey is getting worse day by day'), *Der Tagesspiegel*, 19 January 2017, https://www.tagesspiegel.de/kultur/gorki-chefin-shermin-langhoff-die-lage-in-der-tuerkei-verfinstert-sich-taeglich/19265526.html.

9. Kurt Kister, 'Stramm rechts – und im Parlament' ('Strictly right-wing – and in Parliament'), *Süddeutsche Zeitung*, 23 September 2017, https://www.sueddeutsche.de/politik/zeitgeschichte-wo-strauss-die-wand-waehnte-1.3677377.

10. 'Kampfansage nach Bundestagswahl – AfD-Politiker Gauland über Merkel: "Wir werden sie jagen"' ('Post-Election Call to Arms – AfD politician Gauland on Merkel: "We'll hunt her down"'), *BR*, 24 September 2017, https://www.br.de/bundestagswahl/afd-politiker-gauland-ueber-merkel-wir-werden-sie-jagen-100.html. ('People' is here to be understood in its nationalist sense of *Volk*, i.e. the German people. – *GI*.)

11. Interview with Krista Tippett, 'Arnold Eisen: The opposite of good is indifference', On Being, 21 September 2017, transcript, https://onbeing.org/programs/arnold-eisen-the-opposite-of-good-is-indifference-sep2017/.

6. The Intellectual Cleaning Lady

1. Anand Giridharadas, *Winners Take All: The Elite Charade of Changing the World* (New York: Alfred A. Knopf, 2018), p. 267.

2. Back then I still used the term 'Islamophobia', but I now

prefer to talk about 'anti-Muslim racism'. Elisabeth Wehling provides a useful argument for this in her book *Politisches Framing* ('Political Framing'): 'It's just as well that "phobia" hasn't become a fashionable term in other areas too, e.g. "womenphobia" instead of "misogyny", "Jewphobia" instead of "anti-Semitism", "workerphobia" instead of "anti-labour laws". Islamophobia is more than merely problematic; I think it is dangerous. Anti-Muslim thinking is an attitude, not a clinically defined anxiety disorder, and behaviour directed against Muslims is not an "affect" in the psychological sense. If it were true that it was only directed against violent Muslims – as is repeatedly asserted by people trying to explain the threat Islam poses to Christian culture – why call it *Islam*ophobia?' Elisabeth Wehling, *Politisches Framing: Wie eine Nation sich ihr Denken einredet – und daraus Politik macht* ('Political Framing: How a Nation Talks Itself into What it Believes – and Politicises it') (Cologne: Herbert von Halem, 2016), p. 159. If you'd like to read more on this, here are a few of the many authors and academics who have done extensive research on anti-Muslim racism/Islamophobia: Nasar Meer, Arun Kundnani, Salman Sayyid, Fatima Rajina, Nisha Kapoor, Kehinde Andrews and Aleksandra Lewicki. See, for instance, Yasemin Shooman, 'Between Everyday Racism and Conspiracy Theories: Islamophobia on the German-Language Internet', in *Media and Minorities: Questions on Representation from an International Perspective* (Berlin: Vandenhoeck & Ruprecht, 2016), pp. 136–55.

3. Nesrine Malik, 'Otegha Uwagba: "I've spent my entire life treading around white people's feelings"', *The Guardian*, 14 November 2020, https://www.theguardian.com/books/2020/nov/14/otegha-uwagba-ive-spent-my-entire-life-treading-around-white-peoples-feelings.

4. Paula Akpan, 'Why I'm no longer giving racist marketing campaigns my outrage', *gal–dem*, 11 January 2018, https://gal-dem.com/im-no-longer-giving-racist-marketing-campaigns-outrage/.

5. Claude Steele, *Whistling Vivaldi: How Stereotypes Affect Us and What We Can Do* (New York: W. W. Norton & Co., 2011), pp. 59–61.

6. Friedrich Nietzsche, *Human, All Too Human*, trans. Marion Faber and Stephen Elhmann (London: Penguin, 1994), p. 240.

7. Toni Morrison, 'A Humanist View', from *Portland State University's Oregon Public Speakers Collection*, 'Black Studies Center Public Dialogue, Pt. 2', 30 May 1975, https://www.mackenzian.com/wp-content/uploads/2014/07/Transcript_PortlandState_TMorrison.pdf.

8. Maya Angelou, *I Know Why the Caged Bird Sings* (London: Virago, 1984), pp. 84–5.

9. 'Trump defends using "Chinese virus" label, ignoring growing criticism', *The New York Times*, 19 March 2020, https://www.nytimes.com/2020/03/18/us/politics/china-virus.html

10. Adam Bienkov, 'Boris Johnson called gay men "tank-topped bumboys" and Black people "piccaninnies" with "watermelon smiles"', *Insider*, 9 June 2020, https://www.businessinsider.com/boris-johnson-record-sexist-homophobic-and-racist-comments-bumboys-piccaninnies-2019–6?r=US&IR=T.

11. Lizzie Dearden, 'Islamophobic incidents rose 375% after Boris Johnson compared Muslim women to "letterboxes", figures show', *The Independent*, 2 September 2019, https://www.independent.co.uk/news/uk/home-news/boris-johnson-muslim-women-letterboxes-burqa-islamphobia-rise-a9088476.html

12. Cigdem Akyol, 'Die Angst vor dem belgischen Ackergaul' ('Afraid of the Belgian draught horse'), *Taz*, 8 January 2012, https://taz.de/Thilo-Sarrazin-Dokumentation-im-WDR/!5103736/.

13. All quotes are from my private correspondence with Akyün.

14. Jennifer Rubin, 'Opinion: The media must decode Trump's racism and sexism', *The Washington Post*, 13 August 2020, https://www.washingtonpost.com/opinions/2020/08/13/media-must-decode-trumps-racism-sexism/.

15. Mely Kiyak, 'Der Hass ist nicht neu. Für uns nicht.' ('Hate is nothing new. Not for us.'), Otto Brenner Prize

acceptance speech, 29 November 2016, *Über Medien*, https://
uebermedien.de/10293/der-hass-ist-nicht-neu-fuer-uns-nicht.

16. Laura Bates 'How to be a woman online', *Dazed* Digital, 28
January 2014.

17. Ash Sarkar 'Julie Burchill abused me for being Muslim – yet
she was cast as the victim', *The Guardian*, 16 March 2021,
https://www.theguardian.com/commentisfree/2021/mar/16/
julie-burchill-muslim-islamophobic

18. Twitter, 14 March 2019.

19. 'Muslim woman's hijab ripped off in "racist" attack in
London', *Haaretz*, 6 June 2015, https://www.haaretz.com/
woman-s-hijab-ripped-off-in-london-attack-1.5369875

20. Dylan Collins, 'UK: Arrest made in racist attack
on pregnant woman', *Al Jazeera*, 15 September
2016, https://www.aljazeera.com/news/2016/9/15/
uk-arrest-made-in-racist-attack-on-pregnant-woman

21. This case shows just how important it is not to take the
transgressor's point of view when reporting such incidents.
See 'Angreifer boxt schwangere Frau wegen Kopftuch in den
Bauch' ('Attacker punches pregnant woman in the stomach
because of her hijab'), *Berliner Morgenpost*, 20 March
2019, https://www.morgenpost.de/berlin/polizeibericht/
article216699249/Angreifer-boxt-schwangerer-Frau-wegen-
Kopftuch-in-den-Bauch.html.

22. Gavin Ellis and Denis Muller (2020), 'The proximity filter:
The effect of distance on media coverage of the Christchurch
mosque attacks', *Kōtuitui: New Zealand Journal of Social
Sciences Online*, 15(2), pp. 332–48, https://www.tandfonline.
com/doi/full/10.1080/1177083X.2019.1705358.

23. Matthew Young, 'Boy who grew into evil far-right mass
killer as 49 murdered at prayers', *Daily Mirror*, 15 March
2019, https://www.mirror.co.uk/news/world-news/
new-zealand-shooting-brenton-tarrant-14142703

24. Houssem Ben Lazreg, 'The hypocritical media coverage of the
New Zealand terror attacks', *The Conversation*, 25 March
2019, https://theconversation.com/the-hypocritical-media-
coverage-of-the-new-zealand-terror-attacks-113713

25. 'One in four women have had an abortion. Many people think they don't know someone who has, but #youknowme. So let's do this: if you are also the 1 in 4, let's share it and start to end the shame.' Twitter, 15 May 2019, https://twitter.com/BusyPhilipps/status/1128515490559610881?p=v.

26. Twitter, 16 May 2019, https://twitter.com/saralockeSTFW/status/1128873176912605184.

27. 'Organised Love', re:publica, 4 May 2016, https://www.youtube.com/watch?v=BNLhT5hZaV8&t=1s.

28. Martin Luther King, Jr., 'Address at the Fourth Annual Institute on Nonviolence and Social Change at Bethel Baptist Church', 3 December 1959, https://kinginstitute.stanford.edu/king-papers/documents/address-fourth-annual-institute-nonviolence-and-social-change-bethel-baptist-0.

7. The Right-Wing Agenda

1. Victor Klemperer, *LTI: Notizbuch eines Philologen* ('LTI: A Philologer's Notebook') (Stuttgart: Reclam, 1975), p. 21.

2. Bernhard Pörksen, *Die große Gereiztheit. Wege aus der kollektiven Erregung* ('The Prevailing Irritation: Paths out of Collective Agitation') (Munich: Carl Hanser, 2018), p. 165.

3. Carole Cadwalladr, *TED Talk*, 'Facebook's Role in Brexit – And the Threat to Democracy', 16 April 2019, https://www.ted.com/talks/carole_cadwalladr_facebook_s_role_in_brexit_and_the_threat_to_democracy/transcript#t-886323.

4. According to the journalist Ingrid Brodnig, 'the most important online gatekeepers who are sorting and selecting information for us aren't called the BBC, CNN, *Le Monde* or *The New York Times*. They're called Facebook and Google. Which makes it even more problematic when their technicians pretend that they can't influence the process of information selection which the software they themselves have programmed is carrying out.' *Hass im Netz. Was wir gegen Hetze, Mobbing und Lügen tun können* ('Online Hate Speech: What We Can Do Against Incitement, Bullying and Lies') (Vienna: Brandstätter, 2016), p. 201.

5. Philip Kreißel et al., 'Hate at the touch of a button: Right-wing troll factories and the ecosystem of coordinated hate campaigns online' (London: ISD, 2018), https://www.isdglobal.org/wp-content/uploads/2020/04/Hate-at-the-Push-of-a-Button-ISD.pdf

6. The Alan Turing Institute's Public Policy programme published a new policy briefing on 27 November 2019: 'How much online abuse is there? A systematic review of evidence for the UK', p. 4, https://www.turing.ac.uk/sites/default/files/2019–11/online_abuse_prevalence_full_24.11.2019_-_formatted_0.pdf

7. However, despite hate speech and online racism having been a constant topic of discussion in recent years, Ariadna Matamoros-Fernández and Johan Farkas argue that there is 'a lack of geographical and platform diversity, an absence of researchers' reflexive dialogue with their object of study, and little engagement with critical race perspectives to unpack racism on social media. There is a need for more thorough interrogations of how user practices and platform politics co-shape contemporary racisms.' 'Racism, hate speech, and social media: A systematic review and critique', *Television & New Media*, 22(2) (February 2021), pp. 205–24, https://doi.org/10.1177/1527476420982230.

8. Bertholt Brecht, 'Five Difficulties in Writing the Truth', in Tom Kuhn and Steve Giles, eds, *Brecht on Art and Politics*, trans. Laura Bradley and Tom Kuhn (London: Methuen, 2003), p. 149.

9. Noah Sow, *Deutschland Schwarz Weiß. Der alltägliche Rassismus* ('Germany Black [and] White: Everyday Racism') (Munich: Goldmann, 2009), p. 30 ff.

10. In an interview, sociologist Matthias Quent explained how important it was to describe the attack explicitly as 'right-wing terrorism' as opposed to a 'killing spree': 'The attack had a specific political and social effect. The man clearly wanted to create an atmosphere of fear and terror by carrying out an attack against non-white people, against people of colour, designed to shock, to send a message. The

racially motivated selection of victims increases tensions
between social groups. It highlights and reinforces ethnic
difference and performs them as a reason for violence.
That's why I talk about crimes motivated by prejudice and
hate crimes, as well as about right-wing terrorism.' Vanessa
Vu, 'Die Grenzen zwischen Amok und Terror können
verwischen' ('The blurred line between killing spree and
terrorist attack', *Zeit Online*, 2 January 2019, https://www.
zeit.de/gesellschaft/2019–01/rechtsextremismus-anschlag-
bottrop-rassismus-radikalisierung-terror-matthias-quent/
komplettansicht.

11. *exit RACISM*, p. 75.

12. Alexander Gauland said this during ARD's 'Sommerinterview'
on 15 September 2019: Gauland – 'But some among us forget
that our party is an action group [...]'. Host – 'An action
group?' Gauland – 'An action group in terms of political
change, and having access to political power.' See https://
www.youtube.com/watch?v=rv5TrBrg73w.

13. As Edward Sapir said: 'The word is merely a form, a
definitely molded entity that takes in as much or as little of
the conceptual material of the whole thought as the genius
of the language cares to allow.' Edward Sapir, *Language: An
Introduction to the Study of Speech* (Harcourt, Brace & Co.,
1921).

14. Twitter, 15 March 2021, https://twitter.com/realchrisrufo/
status/1371540368714428416

15. Twitter, 15 March 2021, https://twitter.com/realchrisrufo/
status/1371541044592996352

16. Donald J. Trump, 'A plan to get divisive & radical theories
out of our schools', RealClear Politics, 18 June 2021, https://
www.realclearpolitics.com/articles/2021/06/18/a_plan_to_get_
divisive__radical_theories_out_of_our_schools_145946.html

17. Lawrence Richard, 'Ted Cruz slams critical race theory as
"every bit as racist as the klansmen in white sheets"', Yahoo!
News, 18 June 2021, https://news.yahoo.com/ted-cruz-slams-
critical-race-185300323.html

18. Ed Kilgore, 'Why Republicans want voters to panic about

critical race theory,' *New York Magazine*, 24 June 2021, https://nymag.com/intelligencer/article/republicans-voters-panic-critical-race-theory.html

19. Ibram X. Kendi, 'There is no debate over critical race theory', *The Atlantic*, 9 July 2021, https://www.theatlantic.com/ideas/archive/2021/07/opponents-critical-race-theory-are-arguing-themselves/619391/

20. US Senator Tom Cotton on Twitter, 13 August 2021: 'It's clear President Biden and his Department of Defense have been more concerned with critical race theory and other woke policies than planning an orderly withdrawal from Afghanistan', https://twitter.com/SenTomCotton/status/1426162752469483531

21. Sana Saeed on Twitter, 21 August 2021. 'Instead of using this moment to earnestly self-reflect on the criminal excesses of the War in Afghanistan, on the toll it took on the ppl of Afghanistan, the US media collectively erased twenty years of history & rewrote the narrative to make the US a restrained savior', https://twitter.com/SanaSaeed/status/1429135147366948871

22. https://www.theguardian.com/politics/2016/jun/16/nigel-farage-defends-ukip-breaking-point-poster-queue-of-migrants

23. Victor Klemperer, *LTI: Notizbuch eines Philologen*, p. 256.

24. Ron Suskind, 'Faith, certainty and the presidency of George W. Bush', *The New York Times*, 17 October 2004, https://www.nytimes.com/2004/10/17/magazine/faith-certainty-and-the-presidency-of-george-w-bush.html.

8. The Illusion of Sovereignty

1. Aristotle, *Categories*, trans. E. M. Edghill, in J. A. Smith and W. D. Ross, *The Works of Aristotle*, I.5 (Oxford: Clarendon Press, 1928).

2. Michel Foucault, *The Will to Knowledge: The History of Sexuality*, vol. 1, trans. Robert Hurley (London: Penguin, 1998), p. 95.

3. Bargh, *Before You Know It*. For full details see Lawrence E. Williams and John A. Bargh, 'Experiencing physical warmth

promotes interpersonal warmth', *Science*, 24 October 2008, 322(5901), pp. 606–7, https://www.ncbi.nlm.nih.gov/pmc/articles/PMC2737341.

4. Mareike Nieberding, 'Was Frauen krank macht' ('What makes women ill'), *Süddeutsche Zeitung*, 23 May 2019, https://sz-magazin.sueddeutsche.de/frauen/frauengesundheit-medizin-87304?reduced=true.

5. Among the areas of women's health that have been thoroughly researched are contraception (e.g. the contraceptive pill) and depression. Depression is an area in which men have been neglected, despite the fact that the suicide rate is higher in men than women. In this case, too, gaps in the data can clearly be fatal.

6. *Invisible Women*, pp. xi–xiii.

7. Bernd Ulrich, *Guten Morgen, Abendland. Der Westen am Beginn einer neuen Epoche: Ein Weckruf* ('Good morning, Occident: The West at the Beginning of a New Era – a Wake-up Call') (Cologne: Kiepenheuer & Witsch, 2017), p. 27.

8. See Thomas Bauer, *Kultur der Ambiguität* ('The Culture of Ambiguity') (Berlin: Insel, 2011), pp. 251 and 312, and Friedrich Nietzsche, *On the Genealogy of Morals*, trans. Douglas Smith (Oxford: Oxford World's Classics, 1998), p. 98.

9. Friedrich Nietzsche, *The Joyous Science*, trans. R. Kevin Hill (London: Penguin, 2018), p. 281.

10. Bauer, p. 27.

11. Ibid., p. 251.

12. Ibid., p. 250.

13. Ibid., p. 344.

14. Ibid, p. 346 ff.

15. Ibid., p. 347.

9. Speaking Freely

1. Cited by Peter M. Senge in his preface to David Bohm, *On Dialogue* (Abingdon: Routledge Classics, 2004), p. xi.

2. The 'contact hypothesis' was first proposed by the

psychologist Gordon W. Allport in his book *The Nature of Prejudice* (Reading, MA: Perseus Books, 1954).

3. Chimamanda Ngozi Adichie, 'The Danger of a Single Story', *TED Global 2009*, https://www.ted.com/talks/chimamanda_ngozi_adichie_the_danger_of_a_single_story/transcript?language=en#t-699439 (10:43).

4. 'Abla' is a Turkish term used to respectfully address women (slightly) older than you. It literally translates as 'big sister'.

5. James Baldwin, 'Stranger in the Village', *Notes of a Native Son* (London: Penguin, 2017), pp. 165–6.

6. Alexandra Wilson on Twitter, 23 September 2020, https://twitter.com/EssexBarrister/status/1308854340258598913.

7. Jacob Sam-La Rose, *Sable LitMag*, Autumn 2002, p. 60.

8. *Plantation Memories*, p. 12.

9. Viet Thanh Nguyen, Twitter, https://twitter.com/viet_t_nguyen/status/1100788236824109056 (27 February 2019) and https://twitter.com/viet_t_nguyen/status/1100993739235909633 (28 February 2019).

10. The scholar Saboura Manpreet Naqshband uses 'critical potatoism' to describe 'white Germans who are anti-racist in their thinking and behaviour, and can laugh at the customs and traditions of their culture. It also describes those who, for the sake of collective well-being, genuinely (want to) engage with the racist present and past'. See https://instagram.com/p/B2rQJ8forhT.

11. First broadcast online in early 2018, the programme was initially called *BlackRock Talk* ('black rock' being the literal English translation of its founder Esra Karakaya's surname). In October 2019, it moved to ARD and ZDF's youth channel, *funk*, and its name was changed to *Karakaya Talk*. In May 2020, Karakaya announced that *funk* and *Karakaya Talk* would part ways. See https://www.deutschlandfunk.de/wo-bleibt-das-diverse-talk-format-empathie-ist-nichts.807.de.html?dram:article_id=491945.

12. *Derry Girls*, Channel 4, Season 1, Episode 1, first aired 4 January 2018 (3:50).

13. *For the Record*, p. 64.

14. Kartina Richardson, 'How can white Americans be free? The default belief that the white experience is a neutral and objective one hurts both white and American culture', *Salon*, 25 April 2013 (https://www.salon.com/213/04/25/how_can_white_americans_be_free).

15. I keep hearing white, privileged artists, musicians and writers telling marginalised people with apparent envy that they are 'lucky' to have suffered, having thereby acquired 'material' for their art. This is a particularly good example of ignorance masquerading as understanding, because every marginalised artist I know would gladly give up their work if it meant the end of oppression. But this is not what the author meant that evening.

16. Ghayath Almadhoun, 'The Capital', trans. Catherine Cobham, http://www.citybooks.eu/en/cities/citybooks/p/detail/the-capital.

10. A New Way of Speaking

1. Lewis Carroll, *Alice's Adventures in Wonderland* (Boston: Lee & Shepard, 1869), p. 89.

2. Aladin El-Mafaalani, *Das Integrationsparadox. Warum gelungene Integration zu mehr Konflikten führt* ('The Integration Paradox: Why Successful Integration Leads to Increased Conflict) (Cologne: Kiepenheuer & Witsch, 2018).

3. More than thirty years ago, the political scientist Helga Körnig described a similar conflict in her essay 'Als "Vorzimmerdame" begehrt – als Kollegin unerwünscht!' ('A desirable receptionist – an unwanted colleague!'), but with regard to the role of (white) women. Which serves as a reminder that some battles are only 'new' on the face of it. See Marlies Fröse (ed.), *Utopos – Kein Ort: Mary Daly's Patriarchatskritik und feministische Politik; ein Lesebuch* ('Utopos – No Place: Mary Daly's Criticism of the Patriarchy and Feminist Politics: A Reader') (Bielefeld: AJZ, 1988).

4. *Das Integrationsparadox*, pp. 79 and 229.

5. The then US president Donald Trump tweeted something

along those lines in July 2019 about four Democrat
Congresswomen of colour. His tweets caused outrage.

6. Marvin E. Milbauer, 'Powell, King Speak on Negro
Problems', *Harvard Crimson*, 25 April 1964, https://www.
thecrimson.com/article/1964/4/25/powell-king-speak-on-
negro-problems. For a clip of the speech see https://www.
youtube.com/watch?v=o_WJ4PpxWaE (12'06").

7. Naika Foroutan, *Die postmigrantische Gesellschaft: Ein
Versprechen der pluralen Demokratie* ('Post-migrant Society:
A Promise of Pluralist Democracy') (Bielefeld: Transcript,
2019), p. 13 ff.

8. Article 7, https://www.un.org/en/about-us/
universal-declaration-of-human-rights.

9. Article 14, https://www.legislation.gov.uk/ukpga/1998/42/
schedule/1/enacted.

10. 'Media watch: Celebrating women's words', *New Directions
for Women*, 15(3) (1986), p. 6.

11. Erik Olin Wright, *Envisioning Real Utopias* (London: Verso,
2010), p. 370. In his discussion of utopias, Wright argues that
'*Capitalism obstructs the realization of both social justice
and political justice.* This is the fundamental starting point
in the search for alternatives: the critique of capitalism as a
structure of power and inequality. [...] This does not imply
that all social injustices are attributable to capitalism, nor
does it imply that the complete elimination of capitalism is
a necessary condition for significant advances in social and
political justice. But it does imply that the struggle for human
emancipation requires a struggle against capitalism, not
simply a struggle within capitalism.' Ibid., pp. 366–7.

12. Foucault called such spaces 'heterotopias': 'real places –
places that do exist and that are formed in the very founding
of society – which are something like counter-sites, a kind
of effectively enacted utopia in which the real sites, all the
other real sites that can be found within the culture, are
simultaneously represented, contested, and inverted. Places
of this kind are outside of all places, even though it may be
possible to indicate their location in reality.' Michel Foucault,

'Of other spaces', trans. Jay Miskowiec, *Diacritics*, 16(1) (Spring 1986), pp. 22–7 (24).

13. Wright, *Envisioning Real Utopias*, p. 370.

14. Rainer Maria Rilke, letter to Franz Xaver Kappus, 16 July 1903, *Briefe an einen jungen Dichter* ('Letters to a Young Poet') (Insel, Leipzig, 1929), p. 23.

15. Carolin Emcke, 'Raus bist du' ('You're out'), *Süddeutsche Zeitung*, 13 May 2019, https://www.sueddeutsche.de/politik/carolin-emcke-kolumne-rassismus-1.4439103.

16. Kimberlé Williams Crenshaw, 'Demarginalizing the intersection of race and sex: A black feminist critique of antidiscrimination doctrine, feminist theory and antiracist politics', *University of Chicago Legal Forum*, 1989(1), https://chicagounbound.uchicago.edu/uclf/vol1989/iss1/8.

17. *On Dialogue*, p. 7.

18. David Bohm, *Unfolding Meaning: A Weekend of Dialogue* (London: Routledge, 1985), p. 175.

19. Robert Jones Jr, Twitter, 18 August 2015, https://twitter.com/SonofBaldwin/status/633644373423562753. In early November 2020 Jones explained the specific context of his tweet, and added: 'If you are retweeting this tweet, please understand that as universal as it sounds pulled out of its context, it was, in fact, intended as a balm and rallying call for Black people in particular, tied especially to our struggles externally and internally. In other words: This a Black quote with Black intent and Black impact for Black people. It's great if you find some universality in it, but recognize its core is Black. Thank you.' Twitter, 8 November 2020, https://twitter.com/SonofBaldwin/status/1325516933178028032.

20. *For the Record*, p. 211.

21. Anand Giridharadas, 'Democracy is not a supermarket: Why real change escapes many change-makers – and why it doesn't have to', 1 November 2017, @AnandWrites, https://medium.com/@AnandWrites/why-real-change-escapes-many-change-makers-and-why-it-doesnt-have-to-8e4832042a8.

22. Roxane Gay, *Bad Feminist* (London: Corsair, 2014), pp. 4 and 318.

23. Simone Weil, 'Attention and Will', in *Gravity and Grace*, trans. Emma Craufurd (London: Routledge and Kegan Paul, 1952).
24. *The Qu'ran*, trans. M. A. S. Abdel Haleem (Oxford: OUP, 2015), p. 258.